HEALING YOUR ANXIOUS ATTACHMENT

HEALING YOUR ANXIOUS ATTACHMENT

BUILD HEALTHY AND SECURE RELATIONSHIPS BY CONQUERING INSECURITY AND YOUR FEAR OF ABANDONMENT

LAURA COLLINS

Teilingen
PRESS

Copyright © 2024 by Laura Collins

All rights reserved. No part of this book may be reproduced, stored in a retrieval system, or transmitted in any form or by any means, electronic, mechanical, photocopying, recording, or otherwise, without the prior written permission of the publisher, Teilingen Press.

The information contained in this book is based on the author's personal experiences and research. While every effort has been made to ensure the accuracy of the information presented, the author and publisher cannot be held responsible for any errors or omissions.

This book is intended for general informational purposes only and is not a substitute for professional medical, legal, or financial advice. If you have specific questions about any medical, legal, or financial matters matters, you should consult with a qualified healthcare professional, attorney, or financial advisor.

Teilingen Press is not affiliated with any product or vendor mentioned in this book. The views expressed in this book are those of the author and do not necessarily reflect the views of Teilingen Press.

This book is for anyone who has struggled with anxious attachment in one way or another. I dedicate these words to your bravery and strength as you embark on the path to healing.

To those searching for security in relationships, I hope this book can be a guide. Your courage to be vulnerable and seek guidance is noticed and appreciated—it's what helps build real connections.

Connection is why we're here; it is what gives purpose and meaning to our lives

BRENÉ BROWN

CONTENTS

Introduction	xiii
1. THE SCIENCE OF ATTACHMENT	1
Anxious Attachment in Infancy	4
Brain Chemistry and Attachment	5
Comparison with Other Attachment Styles	6
Case Studies	7
Chapter Summary	9
2. IDENTIFYING ANXIOUS ATTACHMENT	11
Self-Assessment Techniques	12
When to Seek Help	14
Common Misconceptions	16
Chapter Summary	17
3. ROOT CAUSES OF ANXIOUS ATTACHMENT	19
Parental Influence	19
Traumatic Events	20
Genetic Factors	21
Early Childhood Environment	23
Educational Impact	24
Chapter Summary	25
4. CONSEQUENCES OF ANXIOUS ATTACHMENT	29
In Romantic Relationships	30
In Friendships	31
At Work	32
Mental Health Outcomes	34
Physical Health Implications	36
Social Isolation	37
Chapter Summary	38

5. THERAPEUTIC APPROACHES — 41
   Cognitive Behavioral Therapy — 41
   Dialectical Behavior Therapy — 42
   Psychodynamic Therapy — 44
   Couples Therapy — 45
   Group Therapy — 46
   Online Therapy — 48
   Chapter Summary — 49

6. SELF-HELP STRATEGIES — 51
   Building Self-Esteem — 51
   Creating Boundaries — 52
   Emotional Regulation Techniques — 54
   Journaling — 57
   Chapter Summary — 58

7. NAVIGATING RELATIONSHIPS — 61
   Attachment Styles in Partners — 62
   Communication Patterns — 64
   Rebuilding Trust — 65
   Handling Conflicts — 67
   Maintaining Independence — 68
   Chapter Summary — 70

8. SUPPORT AND RESOURCES — 73
   Finding the Right Therapist — 73
   Support Groups and Communities — 75
   Books and Online Resources — 76
   Apps and Tools — 78
   Emergency Assistance — 79
   Chapter Summary — 80

9. PERSONAL GROWTH AND DEVELOPMENT — 83
   Setting Personal Goals — 83
   Learning New Skills — 85
   Embracing Change — 85
   Your Self-Discovery Journey — 87
   Celebrating Successes — 88
   Chapter Summary — 89

10. CASE STUDIES AND REAL-LIFE EXAMPLES   91
    Case Study 1: Individual Therapy   91
    Case Study 2: Couples Therapy   93
    Case Study 3: Self-Help Success   94
    Case Study 4: Relapse and Recovery   96

11. CULTURAL PERSPECTIVES   99
    Global Variations in Therapy Approaches   101
    Cultural Stigma and Mental Health   102
    Cultural Acceptance of Self-Help   104
    Cross-Cultural Relationships   105
    Immigration and Attachment   107
    Chapter Summary   108

12. FUTURE DIRECTIONS   111
    Innovative Therapies   112
    Technology and Mental Health   114
    Educational Programs   115
    Policy and Mental Health   116
    Global Mental Health Initiatives   118
    Chapter Summary   120

    Epilogue   123

    Your Feedback Matters   131
    About the Author   133

INTRODUCTION

Anxious attachment is a term that often pops up when we talk about relationships and how we connect with others. But what does it really mean?

At its core, anxious attachment is a style of interpersonal relationship where someone exhibits a high level of insecurity and worries about being rejected or abandoned. This attachment style is rooted in early childhood experiences, typically shaped by interactions with caregivers.

Imagine a child who never knows if their cry will bring a comforting embrace or if their achievements will be met with enthusiasm or indifference. This inconsistency can lead to a heightened sensitivity to the moods and behaviors of others, which can carry over into adult relationships. People with an anxious attachment style often find themselves in a perpetual state of alert, constantly on the lookout for signs that their relationship might be in jeopardy.

This hyper-vigilance can manifest in several ways. For instance, someone might excessively seek reassurance from

INTRODUCTION

their partners, have difficulty enjoying moments of closeness because they fear it won't last, or even misinterpret neutral actions as negative. It's like having an internal alarm system that is too sensitive, where even the slightest trigger can set off anxiety and fear of loss.

Understanding anxious attachment is crucial not just for those who live with it but also for their partners and loved ones. Recognizing the signs can lead to more supportive, empathetic interactions and can help build a foundation for security and trust in relationships.

IMPORTANCE OF ATTACHMENT STYLES

Understanding attachment styles is crucial because they influence how we form and maintain relationships. It's also about paving the way for personal growth and healthier interactions. By identifying and addressing the roots of our attachment styles, we can work towards forming more secure and fulfilling connections with others.

Moreover, this understanding can enhance our empathy towards others, helping us see the underlying reasons for their relationship behaviors. This can lead to more compassionate interactions and a better support system for those struggling with the effects of their attachment styles.

For example, people with an anxious attachment style often experience a deep fear of abandonment, which can lead to behaviors that paradoxically push others away. As adults, individuals with this style may find themselves continuously seeking reassurance from partners, friends, and family, which can strain relationships.

In essence, delving into attachment styles equips us with

the tools to improve our relational patterns and foster a more understanding and supportive environment. This knowledge is invaluable as it touches every aspect of our interactions and the quality of our connections with others.

GOALS OF THIS BOOK

In this book, our primary goal is to demystify the concept of anxious attachment and provide you with a clear understanding of how it influences relationships and personal growth. We will explore the characteristics, causes, and effects of anxious attachment, offering insights into how it can manifest in various aspects of life, including romantic relationships, friendships, and professional interactions.

We will also provide practical strategies for managing anxious attachment. This includes techniques for self-awareness, improving communication skills, and fostering healthier relationships. By the end of this book, you should feel equipped with the tools to identify signs of anxious attachment in yourself and others and take steps towards more loving and lasting connections.

This book also hopes to foster a supportive community. By sharing knowledge and experiences, we can help each other understand and overcome the challenges associated with anxious attachment. Whether you are directly affected by anxious attachment or know someone who is, this book will offer valuable perspectives and solutions to improve your interpersonal dynamics and emotional well-being.

INTRODUCTION

HOW TO USE THIS BOOK

This book is designed to be a practical resource, whether you're someone who identifies with an anxious attachment style, a therapist, or simply a curious reader seeking to understand more about attachment in relationships.

To get the most out of this book, start at the beginning and progress through each section sequentially. The early chapters lay a foundation for understanding anxious attachment and its historical context, which is crucial for grasping the more detailed discussions in later sections.

Each chapter includes explanations, real-life examples, and research findings to help solidify the concepts discussed. These are intended to help you apply the knowledge to your own life, fostering a deeper understanding and facilitating personal growth.

Feel free to take your time with each section. Reflect on the insights and how they resonate with your experiences or observations of others. Consider how the information might help your work with clients if you're a therapist.

Lastly, I encourage you to use the summary points at the end of each chapter to review key concepts before moving on. This will reinforce your learning and ensure you have a solid grasp of the information before proceeding to the next chapter.

This book is not just a read; it's an interactive tool designed to engage you in a journey of understanding and self-discovery. So, dive in, reflect, and explore the dynamics of anxious attachment.

CHAPTER SUMMARY

- Anxious attachment is a relationship style characterized by insecurity and fear of rejection, often rooted in inconsistent early childhood experiences with caregivers.
- Individuals with anxious attachment remain highly sensitive to others' moods and behaviors, constantly fearing relationship instability.
- This attachment style can lead to behaviors like excessive reassurance-seeking and misinterpreting neutral actions as negative due to an overly sensitive internal alarm system.
- Understanding anxious attachment is crucial as it influences adult relationship dynamics and behaviors, often leading to a cycle of insecurity and relationship strain.
- The book aims to provide a comprehensive understanding of anxious attachment, exploring its characteristics, causes, and effects on personal and professional relationships.
- It will provide practical strategies for managing anxious attachment, including improving self-awareness, communication skills, and fostering healthier relationships.
- The book is structured as a practical guide, offering real-life examples, research findings, and guidance to help you apply the knowledge to your life.

CHAPTER 1
THE SCIENCE OF ATTACHMENT

Let's dive into the basics of attachment theory. It's a cornerstone concept that helps us understand the development of emotional bonds between individuals. We can trace its origins back to the mid-20th century with the pioneering work of British psychologist John Bowlby. Bowlby, the father of attachment theory, first introduced the idea that the bonds formed between children and their primary caregivers have profound impacts that extend well into adulthood. His research was groundbreaking, suggesting that these early attachment styles shape our relationships and emotional patterns throughout our lives.

According to Bowlby, attachment behaviors are instinctive, triggered by conditions threatening proximity to the caregiver, such as separation or insecurity. Bowlby's work was further developed by his colleague, Mary Ainsworth, who introduced the concept of the "Strange Situation" — a procedure used to observe the nature of attachment between infants and their caregivers. Through her work, Ainsworth identified three main styles of attachment: secure, avoidant, and anxious-ambivalent (often called 'anxious'). A fourth attachment style, disorganized attachment, was identified by later researchers.

Secure Attachment

Secure attachment in children is characterized by confidence that their caregivers will meet their needs. They show distress when separated but are quickly comforted upon their return. As adults, individuals with secure attachments tend to have healthy, balanced relationships marked by trust, emotional closeness, and effective communication.

Avoidant Attachment

Avoidant attachment in children is marked by indifference to their caregivers' presence or absence, and they show little emotional response when they leave or return. In adulthood, this manifests as a tendency to avoid intimacy, maintain emotional distance, and be self-reliant, often struggling with close relationships.

Anxious-Ambivalent Attachment (Anxious Attachment)

Children with anxious attachment showed extreme distress when separated from their caregivers and were ambivalent when they returned, seeking comfort yet simultaneously resisting it. Adults with this attachment style typically exhibit a strong fear of abandonment and a craving for closeness, but they often feel that their need for intimacy is not being met. This attachment style is characterized by high levels of anxiety and uncertainty, often resulting in clingy or needy behaviors.

Disorganized Attachment

Disorganized attachment is characterized by a lack of a coherent attachment style. Children with this attachment style often display confusing and contradictory behaviors, such as approaching the caregiver but with an averted gaze or showing signs of fear toward them. This disorganization typically arises from caregivers who are frightening or frightened themselves, leading to a sense of unpredictability and insecurity. In adulthood, disorganized attachment can manifest as chaotic and unstable relationships, difficulties in regulating emotions, and a pervasive sense of mistrust and fear in close connections.

Understanding these attachment styles and their historical background highlights how deeply embedded attachment is in psychological research. It's not just a contemporary buzzword but a well-studied phenomenon that has evolved over decades. Understanding its origins helps us appreciate the complexity of human relationships and the enduring influence of our earliest interactions.

Attachment theory offers a framework for understanding the diversity in human relationships. It provides insights into how early experiences with caregivers can influence an individual's behavior in romantic relationships, friendships, and even professional interactions. As we explore further, we'll see how these foundational bonds shape us, echoing throughout our lives.

ANXIOUS ATTACHMENT IN INFANCY

When we talk about anxious attachment in infancy, we're diving into how early interactions between a baby and their caregiver can set the stage for how they handle relationships later in life. Anxiously attached infants often show signs of distress and are not easily comforted, even when their caregiver returns after a brief absence. This behavior stems from the infant's experience of inconsistent responsiveness from their caregiver. Sometimes, their needs are met promptly and with great sensitivity, but at other times, the caregiver might be neglectful or overly intrusive.

This inconsistency can be confusing for infants, making it hard for them to develop a secure sense of trust and safety. They become more hyper-vigilant about their caregiver's movements and moods, remaining on an emotional high alert to guard against potential threats of separation or neglect. This state of heightened alertness can be exhausting, not just for the baby but also for the caregiver.

The roots of this attachment style can often be traced back to the caregiver's own attachment history. Caregivers who themselves have unresolved fears and anxieties about attachment tend to pass on these patterns despite their best intentions. They might switch between being overly protective and somewhat disengaged based on their fluctuating capacity to manage their own stress and emotional responses.

Understanding these dynamics is crucial, not only for clinicians and practitioners working with children and families but also for parents themselves. Recognizing the signs of anxious attachment early on can lead to effective interventions that provide both the infant and the caregiver with the tools to develop a more secure attachment. Techniques such as consistent and sensitive responsiveness, learning to read the infant's cues accurately, and self-regulation strategies for the caregiver can significantly alter the attachment trajectory.

The development of an anxious attachment style in infancy highlights the critical impact of early relational experiences. It shows the importance of nurturing a secure, stable, responsive caregiving environment that fosters healthy emotional and social development.

BRAIN CHEMISTRY AND ATTACHMENT

A fascinating interplay of hormones and neurotransmitters influences our emotional and attachment behaviors. Central to this discussion are two key players: cortisol and oxytocin.

Cortisol, often referred to as the "stress hormone," is typically elevated in individuals with anxious attachment styles. This elevation can be traced back to early developmental stages, where consistent stress patterns and unpredictability in caregiver responses lead to a hyperactivation of the hypothalamic-pituitary-adrenal axis. As a result, individuals with an anxious attachment style may experience heightened stress responses and prolonged cortisol secretion, which can affect their overall emotional regulation and stress management.

Oxytocin, the "love hormone," is crucial in forming social

bonds and maintaining close personal relationships. It helps to mitigate stress and promote feelings of calm and connectedness. However, individuals with anxious attachment can have an inconsistent oxytocin response. While they may have a strong initial release of oxytocin, their ongoing insecurity in relationships might disrupt the sustained effects of this hormone, leading to a cycle of intense attachment needs followed by fear of rejection or abandonment.

Understanding these biochemical underpinnings sheds light on why individuals with anxious attachment may behave the way they do. Their biological responses to stress and social bonding are skewed, which perpetuates their cycles of intense emotional responses and fears within relationships.

By recognizing these patterns, individuals and their support network can better address the root causes of anxious attachment, employing strategies that help regulate these chemical responses and foster healthier, more secure attachment behaviors. This insight deepens our understanding of attachment theory and opens avenues for more targeted interventions that can lead to lasting changes in attachment styles.

COMPARISON WITH OTHER ATTACHMENT STYLES

Understanding anxious attachment becomes more apparent when we compare it with other attachment styles. Let's examine how it compares to secure, avoidant, and disorganized attachment styles.

The main difference between secure and anxious attachment lies in the stress response. Individuals with secure attachment tend to approach stress with confidence and stability. They trust that support is available when needed. In contrast, those with anxious attachment often fear abandonment and may exhibit clingy behavior, constantly seeking reassurance from their partners or caregivers.

Next, let's consider avoidant attachment. While individuals with anxious attachment crave closeness, those with avoidant attachment might do the opposite. They typically maintain emotional distance and often perceive intimacy as a threat to their independence. This starkly contrasts with the anxious style, where emotional closeness is not just desired but intensely needed.

Lastly, there is the disorganized attachment style, which involves a mix of behaviors and feelings toward caregivers, including fear, confusion, and longing. This style can sometimes resemble anxious attachment because both involve intense emotions. However, disorganized attachment is more chaotic and lacks the consistent strategy of seeking closeness found in anxious attachment.

Each style shapes how individuals perceive and react to their relationships and environments. By understanding these differences, we can better appreciate the unique challenges and needs associated with anxious attachment.

CASE STUDIES

Let's delve into some real-life scenarios that illustrate the impact of anxious attachment across different stages of life. These case studies bring the theory to life and highlight the lasting effects of early attachment experiences on later relationships and personal development.

First, consider the case of Paula, a 30-year-old accounting executive. Paula's childhood was marked by an emotionally unpredictable mother—affectionate one moment and distant the next. This inconsistency led Paula to become hyper-vigilant about the moods and behaviors of others, constantly seeking approval and reassurance. In her romantic relationships, she often feels insecure and fears abandonment, which drives her to seek constant contact and reassurance from her partners. This pattern has led to a series of tumultuous relationships.

Next, we have the story of Leo, a 25-year-old graduate student who exhibits signs of anxious attachment that stem from his early experiences with his caregivers. His parents, though loving, were often overly protective and inconsistently available, oscillating between smothering affection and complete absorption in their own issues. As a result, Leo struggles with self-esteem and often feels unworthy of love. His relationships are characterized by a fear of being alone, leading him to cling to partners even in unhealthy situations.

Another poignant example is Ava, a 40-year-old teacher who was raised by a single father who struggled with alcoholism. Her father's affection and attention were sporadic and largely dependent on his sobriety. Ava grew up feeling that she needed to earn his love and attention, often feeling anxious and unsure about her worth. This has translated into her adult life as a pattern of anxious attachments, where she often finds herself in relationships where she feels she must "earn" love, mirroring the insecurity she felt as a child.

These case studies reveal how anxious attachment can

manifest and affect personal relationships and self-perception. They highlight the importance of understanding one's attachment style and, where necessary, working towards developing a more secure attachment through therapy, self-awareness, and personal growth. Understanding these patterns is the first step toward change and healing, allowing individuals to forge healthier relationships.

CHAPTER SUMMARY

- Attachment theory, developed by John Bowlby, focuses on the emotional bonds between infants and caregivers, crucial for a child's development and future relationships.
- Mary Ainsworth expanded the theory, identifying three main attachment styles: secure, anxious-ambivalent, and avoidant, through her "Strange Situation" study. Disorganized attachment was later identified as an additional attachment style.
- An anxious attachment style is marked by fear of abandonment and a strong desire for closeness, often resulting in clingy behavior due to unmet intimacy needs.
- Anxious attachment in infancy is characterized by distress and difficulty in comforting, often due to inconsistent caregiver responsiveness, leading to heightened alertness and emotional strain.
- Brain chemistry plays a significant role in anxious attachment, with elevated cortisol levels and

inconsistent oxytocin responses contributing to stress and relationship insecurities.
- Anxious attachment differs from secure (stable and confident), avoidant (emotionally distant), and disorganized (chaotic and fearful) attachment styles.
- Real-life case studies illustrate how early inconsistent caregiving can lead to anxious attachment, affecting adult relationships and self-esteem, highlighting the importance of therapy and self-awareness for improvement.

CHAPTER 2
IDENTIFYING ANXIOUS ATTACHMENT

Recognizing the signs and symptoms of anxious attachment can be a game-changer in understanding one's behavior in relationships. Let's dive into some of the most common indicators.

Firstly, individuals with anxious attachment tend to seek high levels of intimacy and approval from their partners. They might appear overly dependent or clingy, constantly seeking reassurance and validation to overcome their insecurities about the relationship's stability.

Another telltale sign is hypersensitivity to their partner's moods and actions. They are often on high alert for any hint of disinterest or rejection, which can lead to misinterpretations of their partner's behaviors. This sensitivity usually stems from a deep fear that they are not enough and that their partner might leave them.

Communication patterns also reveal a lot about anxious attachment. These individuals may frequently text or call, needing continual contact to feel secure. When they feel ignored or not prioritized, it can trigger intense emotional responses, such as anxiety or anger.

People with anxious attachment often struggle with low self-esteem. They might rely heavily on their relationships to define their self-worth, which makes them particularly vulnerable to feelings of jealousy or competitiveness with their partner's other relationships, including friendships and family ties.

Lastly, their fear of abandonment might lead them to stay in unhealthy or unsatisfying relationships. They may tolerate negative treatment because they believe it's better than being alone, or they might preemptively end relationships to avoid potential pain, even when things are going well.

Understanding these signs and symptoms is crucial not only for those who live with anxious attachment but also for their partners and loved ones. Recognizing these patterns can lead to healthier dynamics and more secure attachments in relationships.

SELF-ASSESSMENT TECHNIQUES

Recognizing whether you have an anxious attachment style is a big step towards understanding your interactions and feelings in close relationships. Here are some self-assessment techniques that can help you identify signs of anxious attachment in yourself:

Reflect on Your Relationship Patterns

Think about your past and current relationships. Do you

often worry that your partners don't love you as much as you love them? Do you find yourself constantly seeking reassurance from them? Writing down these reflections can help you see patterns that might indicate anxious attachment.

Mindfulness and Emotional Awareness

Practicing mindfulness can help you become more aware of your emotional reactions and the thoughts accompanying them. Notice moments when you feel desperate for closeness or fear abandonment. This awareness is key in recognizing anxious attachment behaviors.

Journaling

Start a journal to track your feelings and reactions in relationship contexts. Over time, you might begin to notice trends, such as increased anxiety, when you don't receive immediate responses to texts or calls.

Feedback from Trusted Friends or Family

Sometimes, it's hard to see patterns in ourselves that others might notice easily. Ask close friends or family members about what they observe in your relationship behaviors. Choose people who know you well and whom you trust to give honest, compassionate feedback.

Professional Assessment

Consider speaking with a therapist or counselor who can provide a professional perspective. They can help you explore your attachment style more effectively and offer tools for managing anxious attachment tendencies.

Online Resources and Assessments

While less personalized than other methods, reputable psychological quizzes about attachment styles can offer a starting point for understanding your relationship tendencies.

* * *

By trying these self-assessment techniques, you can gain insights into your attachment style and begin the journey towards healthier, more secure relationships. Remember, the goal isn't to judge yourself harshly but to understand and grow.

WHEN TO SEEK HELP

Recognizing when to seek help for anxious attachment is crucial for your mental health and the quality of your relationships. Consider professional guidance if you are constantly worried about your relationships, fear abandonment, or feel overly needy and clingy.

Firstly, if your anxiety about relationships causes significant distress or interferes with your daily life, this is a clear signal that help is needed. You may notice that you're unable to focus at work or lose sleep over relationship worries. These disruptions are indicators that your attachment anxieties are not just minor concerns but are impacting your overall well-being.

Secondly, if you find yourself in a pattern of unstable relationships, swinging wildly between intense closeness and painful breakups, this might be a manifestation of anxious attachment. Professional counseling can help you understand the roots of these patterns and teach you healthier ways to connect with others.

Suppose your reactions to perceived slights or separations are intense or prolonged, causing you emotional turmoil or leading to behaviors you regret later. This is another sign that seeking help could be beneficial. Sometimes, these reactions are not immediately apparent as overreactions, but it's important to address them if they're causing guilt, shame, or regret.

Seeking help can take various forms, from therapy sessions with a psychologist specializing in attachment issues to joining support groups where you can connect with others facing similar challenges. In later chapters of the book, we'll explore different therapeutic approaches.

Acknowledging the need for help is a sign of strength, not weakness. By seeking support, you're taking a brave step toward building more secure connections. Whether it's through therapy, support groups, or even further education on attachment styles, the important thing is to take action and move towards a healthier emotional life.

COMMON MISCONCEPTIONS

Common misconceptions often cloud our understanding of what anxious attachment truly means.

Misconception # 1: People With Anxious Attachment Are Overly Emotional

One common myth is that individuals with anxious attachment are overly emotional or sensitive. This simplification overlooks the complexity of the attachment style, which is rooted in deeper fears of abandonment and a desperate craving for closeness and security.

Misconception # 2: Anxious Attachment Is Permanent

Another widespread misunderstanding is the belief that anxious attachment is a permanent fixture in someone's personality. From personal experience, I can attest to the transformative power of understanding and addressing one's attachment issues. Years ago, I was constantly anxious in relationships, always looking for signs that something was amiss. It wasn't until I delved into the intricacies of attachment theory and sought professional help that I began to see changes. This journey taught me that with the right interventions and a commitment to self-awareness, change is indeed possible.

Misconception # 3: Anxious Attachment = Dependency

There's also a tendency to confuse anxious attachment

with dependency. While it's true that those with anxious attachment often exhibit dependent behaviors, the core issue is not dependency itself but rather the fear of losing connection. This distinction is crucial for understanding the motivations and behaviors of individuals with this attachment style.

Misconception # 4: Anxious Attachment Only Affects Romantic Relationships

Lastly, it's often assumed that anxious attachment only affects romantic relationships. However, this style can influence many relationships, including friendships, family bonds, and professional interactions. Recognizing this can broaden our approach to therapy and self-improvement, allowing for more comprehensive strategies to manage and heal anxious attachment.

By dispelling these myths, we can approach anxious attachment with a clearer perspective and a better foundation for helping those affected.

CHAPTER SUMMARY

- People with anxious attachment often fear abandonment, leading them to seek high levels of intimacy and approval from partners, appearing clingy or overly dependent.

- They are hypersensitive to their partner's moods and actions, frequently misinterpreting behaviors due to fear of rejection.
- Anxious individuals may engage in frequent communication, such as texting or calling, to feel secure and show intense emotional responses when feeling ignored.
- They often have low self-esteem and rely on relationships to define their self-worth, making them prone to jealousy and staying in unhealthy relationships to avoid loneliness.
- Self-assessment techniques for identifying anxious attachment include reflecting on relationship patterns, practicing mindfulness, journaling, getting feedback from trusted individuals, and professional assessments.
- Seeking help if your anxiety about relationships causes significant distress, leads to unstable relationship patterns, or results in intense emotional reactions.
- Common misconceptions about anxious attachment include it being just oversensitivity, a permanent trait, dependency, and only affecting romantic relationships.

CHAPTER 3
ROOT CAUSES OF ANXIOUS ATTACHMENT

PARENTAL INFLUENCE

Parental influence plays an important role in the development of anxious attachment. From the earliest days of a child's life, the nature of the bond they form with their caregivers sets the stage for their future relationships. This bond, or attachment, is profoundly shaped by the behavior and emotional availability of the parents.

Parents who are consistently warm, responsive, and sensitive to their child's needs tend to foster a secure attachment. However, when parents are inconsistently available—sometimes emotionally present and sometimes not—the child may develop an anxious attachment style. These children often feel unsure if or when their parents will respond to their needs. This inconsistency can lead to anxiety, as the child remains on high alert, trying to ensure they can get the attention and care they crave.

Moreover, parents who are overly anxious themselves can inadvertently pass this trait to their children. Anxious parents may react to their own fears and insecurities by being overly protective or unpredictably responsive. This can be confusing for children about what to expect from others in terms of closeness and support.

The impact of this early parental influence is powerful. Children with anxious attachment often grow up to seek high levels of intimacy and approval from others, constantly fearing rejection or abandonment. They may also display heightened emotional responses and a constant need to maintain relationships, regardless of the personal cost.

Understanding this dynamic is crucial for anyone looking to address and heal from the effects of anxious attachment. Recognizing the role of parental behavior not only helps in healing but also in breaking the cycle with the next generation.

TRAUMATIC EVENTS

Traumatic events can influence the development of anxious attachment styles. When a person experiences a traumatic event, especially during critical developmental periods, it can disrupt their ability to form secure attachments. Trauma can range from a sudden loss of a loved one, witnessing violence, or enduring prolonged absence or inconsistency from primary caregivers. These experiences can instill a persistent fear of abandonment and a sense of insecurity in relationships.

Individuals who have experienced trauma may

constantly seek reassurance from their partners or friends, fearing that if they are not vigilant, they might lose these relationships. This hyper-vigilance is often exhausting, not just for the anxiously attached person but also for those around them. It can lead to a cycle where the more they cling to others, the more pressure they put on their relationships, potentially pushing others away and thus reinforcing their fears of abandonment.

Understanding the link between trauma and anxious attachment is vital. It highlights the importance of addressing past traumas in therapeutic settings to heal these wounds and foster healthier, more secure attachments. Recognizing this connection also helps develop compassion for oneself and others who might be struggling with similar issues. This awareness can be the first step towards breaking the cycle of anxiety and building more stable, meaningful relationships.

GENETIC FACTORS

When exploring the root causes of anxious attachment, it's crucial to consider both environmental and genetic factors. Research suggests that our genes are important in shaping our attachment styles. This doesn't mean that if you have a particular gene, you're predestined to develop anxious attachment, but it does indicate that some people might be more predisposed to it due to their genetic makeup.

Studies involving twins have been particularly enlightening. They show that identical twins, who share the same genetic code, often exhibit more similar attachment styles compared to fraternal twins, who share only about half of their genes. This similarity in attachment styles among identical twins suggests a genetic influence.

Furthermore, scientists have identified specific genes that might influence the development of anxious attachment. For example, variations in the gene coding for the serotonin transporter, which helps regulate mood, have been linked to differences in attachment styles. Individuals with specific variants of this gene might experience higher levels of anxiety and, consequently, might be more likely to develop an anxious attachment style.

It's important to remember that genes are just part of the story. They interact with an individual's environment in complex ways to shape personality and behavior. For instance, a person might have a genetic predisposition for anxious attachment, but if they grow up in a supportive and stable environment, this predisposition might not manifest into an anxious attachment style.

Understanding the genetic components of anxious attachment can be empowering. It helps us recognize that factors beyond our immediate control influence some aspects of our behavior and emotional responses. However, with this knowledge, we can also focus on creating environments that help mitigate these predispositions, whether it's through therapy, building supportive relationships, or other means. This blend of genetic insight and proactive environmental shaping provides a balanced approach to managing and understanding anxious attachment.

EARLY CHILDHOOD ENVIRONMENT

The environment a child grows up in plays a vital role in shaping their attachment style. Certain characteristics of their early childhood environment can be particularly influential for those with anxious attachment. Let's delve into how these environments contribute to the development of anxious attachment.

Firstly, inconsistency in caregiving is a significant factor. Children who experience unpredictable responses from their caregivers—where support and attention are given sporadically—may become anxiously attached. They often remain unsure about when or if their needs will be met, leading to anxiety about their relationships.

Secondly, high levels of conflict or stress within the home can also contribute to this attachment style. Children in these environments are frequently exposed to tense interactions or instability, which can cause them to feel insecure and fearful. As a result, they may develop a sharper sensitivity to the moods and behaviors of others, constantly seeking reassurance and approval to feel safe.

Overprotective parenting can limit a child's ability to explore independently and learn self-regulation. When parents are excessively involved or quick to intervene, children may not learn how to manage their emotions or cope with minor challenges on their own. This can foster a dependency on others for emotional support, a characteristic of anxious attachment.

Cultural factors play a significant role in shaping attachment styles, including the development of anxious attachment. Different cultures have varying expectations and norms surrounding parenting, emotional expression, and interpersonal relationships, all of which can influence how secure or anxious a child's attachment style becomes.

Lastly, a lack of clear boundaries and expectations can confuse children, making it hard for them to develop a secure sense of self. When boundaries are inconsistent, children may feel they must cling to their caregivers to gain any sense of stability, further entrenching anxious attachment behaviors.

Understanding these environmental factors can help address and mitigate the effects of anxious attachment from an early age. By fostering a more stable, supportive, and predictable environment, caregivers can help children develop healthier attachment styles.

EDUCATIONAL IMPACT

We must also consider how school environments and interactions with teachers and peers can influence attachment behaviors. Depending on their experiences, school can either be a place of security and predictability or a source of stress and uncertainty for children with an anxious attachment style.

Children with anxious attachment may display increased sensitivity to their teachers' responses. They might rely heavily on constant feedback and reassurance to feel secure about their social standing and academic performance. This dependency can lead to anxiety if the child perceives any form of criticism or disapproval, even if it's intended to be constructive.

Peer relationships also play a pivotal role. These children might struggle to form and maintain friendships due to their fear of abandonment and rejection. They may exhibit clingy behavior or become overly dependent on certain peers for emotional support, which can strain relationships and lead to social isolation.

The structure of the educational system itself can either exacerbate or alleviate these anxieties. A highly competitive environment emphasizing performance and results may increase stress and insecurity in anxiously attached children. On the other hand, an educational setting that promotes collaboration, emotional learning, and supportive interactions can provide these children with a sense of stability and belonging, helping them develop healthier attachment patterns.

Counseling services, teacher training on attachment issues, and programs that foster a supportive community can be instrumental in educational settings. These resources help educators create an environment that supports emotional and social development, which is crucial for children with anxious attachment styles.

Understanding the educational impact on anxious attachment is vital for developing strategies that support these children in becoming more secure and resilient academically and socially.

CHAPTER SUMMARY

- Parental behavior significantly influences the development of anxious attachment in children.

Inconsistent emotional availability can lead to insecurity and anxiety.
- Anxious parents may pass on their traits to their children through overprotectiveness or unpredictable responses, causing confusion and anxiety in children.
- Traumatic events during critical developmental periods can disrupt secure attachment formation, leading to a persistent fear of abandonment and insecurity in relationships.
- Cultural factors, including societal norms and expectations around parenting and emotional expression, shape attachment styles and can contribute to anxious attachment.
- Genetic predispositions, influenced by specific genes like those coding for serotonin transporters, play a role in the likelihood of developing anxious attachment, though environmental factors also have a significant impact.
- Early childhood environments characterized by inconsistent caregiving, high conflict, overprotectiveness, and unclear boundaries can foster anxious attachment.
- School environments and interactions with teachers and peers significantly impact children with anxious attachment, where a need for constant reassurance can lead to heightened sensitivity and anxiety.
- Educational interventions that promote supportive and collaborative environments can help children

with anxious attachment develop more secure and healthier attachment patterns.

CHAPTER 4
CONSEQUENCES OF ANXIOUS ATTACHMENT

Individuals with anxious attachment often find themselves experiencing a see-saw of emotional highs and lows in relationships.

This attachment style affects not only romantic relationships but also friendships and family dynamics. Anxiously attached individuals often find themselves overly dependent on the approval and presence of their friends or family members, which can strain these relationships. They might frequently seek validation and overreact to perceived slights or distance.

Moreover, the constant stress and anxiety about their relationships can take a toll on their overall mental and emotional health. It's not uncommon for people with this attachment style to experience chronic stress, anxiety, and even depression.

Let's explore how anxious attachment can impact different relationships and aspects of life.

IN ROMANTIC RELATIONSHIPS

When it comes to romantic relationships, individuals with anxious attachment styles often feel intense emotions and insecurity. Their need for closeness can sometimes feel overwhelming, not just to themselves but also to their partners. This intense craving for intimacy stems from deep-rooted fears of abandonment and rejection, fears that are often magnified by the normal ebbs and flows of a relationship.

Imagine a scenario where one partner constantly seeks reassurance from the other. They might text multiple times a day or feel uneasy when their partner is out with friends. This isn't about control or lack of trust but rather an expression of their anxiety about potential loss. The anxious partner may interpret even minor actions as indicators of diminishing affection, leading to miscommunications and arguments.

This increased sensitivity to relational cues also means that individuals with anxious attachment might read too much into minor issues, turning them into bigger conflicts than necessary. They often expect their partners to "just know" how they feel and what they need, leading to disappointment and resentment when those needs aren't met in the expected ways.

On the flip side, when the relationship is stable and their attachment needs are met, individuals with anxious attachment can be exceptionally loving and committed. They often go out of their way to please their partners and make them feel loved, sometimes putting the partner's needs above their own.

However, this dependency on relationship stability to

dictate one's emotional state can be draining for both parties. It places a heavy burden on the relationship to always be the source of happiness and security. In the long run, without conscious effort and communication, this dynamic can lead to burnout for the partner and a perpetuation of anxious behaviors in the individual.

Understanding these patterns is crucial not just for the individual with anxious attachment but also for their partner. Awareness can foster empathy and facilitate a more supportive approach to addressing these insecurities. Through therapy, communication, and mutual understanding, couples can navigate these challenges more effectively, potentially transforming a turbulent relationship into a stable, loving partnership.

IN FRIENDSHIPS

Navigating friendships can be particularly challenging for individuals with anxious attachment styles. Their relationships are often marked by a high need for closeness and an acute fear of abandonment, which can lead to behaviors that strain friendships.

People with anxious attachment might frequently seek reassurance from their friends, needing constant validation that their friendship is secure. This can manifest as frequent texting or calling, an intense desire to spend a lot of time together, and sensitivity to changes in communication patterns or social plans that might be interpreted as rejection or disinterest.

Their intense fear of being alone or disliked can lead them to suppress their true feelings and avoid conflicts. This might seem beneficial in the short term, but over time, it can lead to resentment and a lack of genuine connection, as the relationship is not built on honest and open communication.

Additionally, those with anxious attachment might also struggle with jealousy or possessiveness. Seeing friends spend time with others can trigger a fear that they are being replaced or are no longer valued. This can lead to controlling behaviors, which can push friends away, ironically confirming the anxiously attached individual's fears of abandonment.

The cycle of needing reassurance, fearing abandonment, and reacting in ways that strain the friendship can be exhausting for both parties. It often requires a great deal of patience and understanding from friends and a commitment from the anxiously attached person to work on their attachment issues to foster healthy friendships.

AT WORK

Navigating the professional landscape can be particularly challenging for individuals with an anxious attachment style. These individuals might struggle with a persistent need for reassurance from colleagues and supervisors, which stems from their fear of rejection or criticism. This need can manifest as frequent requests for feedback on their performance, even when reassurance has already been given, or excessive communication, such as repeatedly checking in on project status or seeking feedback more often than necessary.

Those with anxious attachment might interpret neutral or constructive feedback as negative or personal criticism, which can lead to increased stress and sometimes conflict in the workplace. This sensitivity can also make it difficult for them to perform well in environments where feedback is sparse or where they are expected to work independently with little supervision. It can also lead to heightened emotional responses that may seem disproportionate to the situation at hand. Such reactions can confuse colleagues and managers, who might be unaware of the underlying attachment dynamics at play.

Another significant challenge is the handling of professional relationships. Individuals with anxious attachment may find themselves overly reliant on specific coworkers for emotional support, often without realizing it. They might also struggle with jealousy or insecurity when their close colleagues interact with other team members, fearing that their professional relationships might be threatened.

The consequences of anxious attachment can extend to decision-making processes. The intense desire to please and the fear of making mistakes might lead individuals to defer to others' opinions, even when they have valuable insights or alternative ideas that could benefit the project or the organization. This can stifle innovation and personal growth, limiting individual and collective progress.

In team settings, an inherent desire for closeness and approval can lead to overcommitment. They might take on more tasks than they can handle or agree to unrealistic deadlines, all to please their managers and peers. While this can initially seem like a boon to productivity, it's often unsustainable and can lead to burnout.

For example, there was a time when I worked on a team project where one team member, let's call her Sarah, exhibited these anxious tendencies. Sarah would send multiple emails a day asking for reassurance about her work. Initially, it seemed like a diligent follow-up, but it soon became apparent that her actions stemmed from insecurity and a fear of not being 'enough.' This put additional pressure on her and strained the team dynamics as it shifted our focus from the project goals to constantly reassuring her.

However, it's not all challenges. When managed well, individuals with an anxious attachment style can bring a lot of passion and dedication to their roles. Their sensitivity to the needs of others can make them excellent team players and compassionate leaders, provided they receive the support and understanding needed to thrive.

Understanding the dynamics of anxious attachment can lead to more supportive and effective teamwork for employers and colleagues. Simple strategies like providing clear, consistent feedback and recognizing the contributions of anxious attachers can make a significant difference. Encouraging an open communication culture and providing reassurance in times of change or uncertainty can also mitigate some of the stress these individuals may feel.

In conclusion, while anxious attachment can present unique challenges in the workplace, with the right approaches and understanding, individuals with this attachment style can manage and excel in their professional environments.

MENTAL HEALTH OUTCOMES

Living with an anxious attachment style can significantly impact mental health. Individuals with this attachment type often experience a persistent fear of abandonment and rejection, which can lead to a range of emotional and psychological challenges. One of the most common outcomes is anxiety disorders, including generalized anxiety disorder and panic attacks. The constant worry about their relationships can trigger intense episodes of anxiety, which, over time, can become debilitating.

Depression is another frequent consequence. The negative self-view and the chronic stress associated with anxious attachment can erode self-esteem and lead to feelings of hopelessness and sadness. This emotional turmoil can make daily activities and maintaining relationships challenging, further isolating the individual and worsening depressive symptoms.

Moreover, this attachment style can contribute to the development of obsessive-compulsive behaviors. The need for constant reassurance and fear of losing significant relationships can manifest in compulsive checking behaviors, such as repeatedly texting or calling a partner to ensure they haven't lost interest.

Additionally, individuals with an anxious attachment style may struggle with substance abuse. Alcohol or drugs can become a coping mechanism to manage the overwhelming anxiety and emotional pain associated with their attachment insecurities. This, unfortunately, can lead to a cycle of dependency and addiction, compounding their mental health issues.

Understanding these potential mental health outcomes is crucial for those with an anxious attachment style. Recognizing the signs and seeking appropriate help can lead to better management of these challenges, improving overall well-being and quality of life.

PHYSICAL HEALTH IMPLICATIONS

It's not just the emotional and mental aspects of a person's life that are affected by anxious attachment. There's a tangible impact on physical health, too. Individuals with anxious attachment often experience heightened stress responses. This is more than just feeling jittery before a big meeting or date. It's a chronic state where the body frequently activates stress responses, even in non-threatening situations.

This constant state of alert can lead to a series of health issues. For starters, there's the cardiovascular toll. Increased heart rate and blood pressure might not seem like a big deal in the short term, but over the years, this can lead to heart disease, one of the leading causes of death globally.

Then there's the immune system. Have you ever noticed how you're more likely to catch a cold when stressed? That's because stress hormones can suppress the immune system, making you more vulnerable to infections.

Furthermore, the sleep disturbances that often accompany anxious attachment can exacerbate these health problems. Poor sleep doesn't just make you cranky; it's linked to various health issues, from obesity to weakened immune function.

And let's not forget the gastrointestinal system. Stress can disrupt the gut, leading to symptoms ranging from stomachaches to more severe conditions like irritable bowel syndrome.

The physical health implications of anxious attachment underscore the importance of addressing attachment issues. It's not just about feeling better emotionally; it's about preventing serious health conditions that can arise from prolonged stress and anxiety.

SOCIAL ISOLATION

Individuals with anxious attachment often find themselves grappling with social isolation, a consequence that can be both a cause and an effect of their attachment style. This isolation typically stems from their intense fear of rejection and overwhelming desire for closeness, which paradoxically pushes others away, leading to a self-fulfilling prophecy of loneliness.

Imagine someone who constantly seeks reassurance from friends, needing to know they are valued and loved. Over time, this can wear on relationships, causing friends to pull back to avoid the emotional drain. This, in turn, heightens the individual's fears, potentially leading to even clingier behavior. This cycle can spiral, resulting in significant social withdrawal as the person with anxious attachment anticipates rejection even before attempting new relationships.

Social isolation isn't just about physical aloneness but also emotional isolation. People with anxious attachment might be surrounded by others yet feel utterly alone because they perceive their emotional needs as unmet. They might attend parties or social gatherings and interact with others, but the internal experience is one of isolation and disconnection.

This sense of isolation can have profound implications for mental health. It is often associated with increased anxiety, depression, and a sense of helplessness. The loneliness that ensues from being socially isolated can exacerbate the fears at the heart of anxious attachment, creating a challenging cycle to break.

Breaking this cycle often requires therapeutic interventions focusing on building self-esteem, improving communication skills, and fostering greater self-sufficiency. Therapy can also help individuals recognize and modify the patterns of thinking and behavior that lead to social isolation, encouraging more secure and healthy ways of relating to others.

While social isolation is a significant challenge for those with anxious attachment, understanding its dynamics and addressing its root causes can pave the way for more fulfilling and connected lives.

CHAPTER SUMMARY

- Individuals with anxious attachment styles often experience intense emotions and insecurity in romantic relationships, driven by fears of abandonment and rejection.
- Anxiously attached individuals may seek constant reassurance from their partners, misinterpret minor actions as signs of decreased affection, and struggle with communication, leading to conflicts.
- In friendships, people with anxious attachment often need frequent validation, may suppress their true feelings to avoid conflicts, and can exhibit jealousy, potentially straining relationships.
- Anxiously attached individuals may require constant reassurance and struggle with feedback

at work, which can potentially affect their performance and relationships with colleagues.
- Anxious attachment can lead to mental health issues such as anxiety disorders, depression, obsessive-compulsive behaviors, and substance abuse.
- Physically, anxious attachment can cause heightened stress responses, leading to cardiovascular issues, weakened immune function, sleep disturbances, and gastrointestinal problems.
- Socially, anxious attachment often results in isolation due to a fear of rejection and an overwhelming need for closeness, which paradoxically pushes others away.
- Addressing anxious attachment involves therapy, improved communication, and fostering self-sufficiency to break cycles of insecurity and improve well-being.

CHAPTER 5
THERAPEUTIC APPROACHES

COGNITIVE BEHAVIORAL THERAPY

Cognitive Behavioral Therapy (CBT) is a highly effective treatment approach for those grappling with anxious attachment. This therapy focuses on identifying and changing negative thought patterns and behaviors that contribute to anxiety in relationships. CBT helps individuals develop healthier, more secure attachment styles by addressing these cognitive distortions.

The process begins with therapists helping clients to recognize the thoughts that trigger anxiety in relationships. For example, a person might believe that their partner is losing interest if they do not respond immediately to a text. CBT challenges such automatic thoughts and helps the individual to replace them with more realistic and balanced ones.

Therapists also work with clients on behavioral experiments. These small, manageable tasks encourage individuals to gradually face their fears about attachment and relationships. For instance, a therapist might encourage a client to wait a bit longer each time before responding to a partner's messages, helping them to tolerate uncertainty and build confidence in the stability of their relationships.

CBT includes skills training, such as communication and problem-solving skills, which are crucial for building and maintaining healthy relationships. These skills help individuals express their needs and concerns effectively, without fear or anxiety, promoting a healthier interaction pattern with others.

CBT provides a supportive framework that empowers individuals with anxious attachment to better understand their emotions, challenge their fears, and develop healthier ways of connecting with others. Through consistent practice, individuals can experience significant improvements in their relationships and overall well-being.

DIALECTICAL BEHAVIOR THERAPY

Dialectical Behavior Therapy (DBT) is a powerful therapeutic tool that is also effective for individuals with anxious attachment. Originally developed to treat borderline personality disorder, DBT has proven its efficacy in addressing a range of emotional dysregulation issues, including those stemming from anxious attachment styles.

At its core, DBT focuses on four key skill sets: mindfulness, distress tolerance, emotion regulation, and interpersonal effectiveness. Each of these areas is crucial for individuals who experience intense emotions and fears of abandonment, which are common in anxious attachment.

Mindfulness is foundational in DBT. It is practicing being fully present and engaged in the moment without judgment. Mindfulness helps individuals with anxious attachment break the cycle of worrying about past interactions or fearing future abandonment by bringing their focus to the present moment. This skill is vital in managing the overwhelming emotions that can arise in close relationships.

Distress tolerance is particularly beneficial when emotions become too difficult to bear. Instead of resorting to impulsive behaviors to relieve distress, DBT teaches techniques for surviving emotional crises without worsening the situation. These skills are essential for those with anxious attachment, who may experience intense emotional responses to perceived or actual threats in relationships.

Emotion regulation is another critical component of DBT. It helps individuals understand, accept, and manage their emotions effectively. For someone with an anxious attachment style, learning to regulate emotions can reduce the intensity of reactions to abandonment triggers and improve their sense of emotional stability.

Lastly, interpersonal effectiveness skills equip individuals with strategies to communicate more effectively, assert their needs, and handle conflicts without damaging their relationships. These skills are essential for those with anxious attachment, as they often fear that asserting needs will lead to rejection or abandonment.

By integrating these different skills, DBT provides a structured approach to help those with anxious attachment develop healthier, more secure ways of relating to others. It addresses the symptoms and gets to the root of emotional suffering, fostering a greater sense of personal security and more robust, resilient relationships.

PSYCHODYNAMIC THERAPY

Psychodynamic therapy delves into the emotional world of individuals with anxious attachment. This therapeutic approach focuses on uncovering the deep-seated roots of emotional suffering, which often stem from early relational patterns and unresolved conflicts. For those grappling with anxious attachment, psychodynamic therapy can be particularly illuminating, as it explores how early attachments influence current relationships and self-perception.

The process begins by building a therapeutic alliance based on trust. This relationship becomes a cornerstone for exploring past experiences and their emotional residues. Through sessions that often involve discussions about dreams, fantasies, and day-to-day interactions, therapists help individuals uncover the unconscious patterns that dictate their attachment behaviors.

One of the key benefits of psychodynamic therapy is its focus on emotional insight and self-awareness. By understanding the origins of their fears and anxieties, individuals can begin to address these issues in a safe and supportive environment. The therapy not only delves into how these patterns were formed but also provides a space to experiment with new ways of relating to others and oneself.

Psychodynamic therapy also addresses the way individuals with an anxious attachment may idealize or devalue others, a process known as splitting. This understanding helps in managing emotions more effectively and fosters healthier relationships. The ultimate goal is to develop a more secure and coherent sense of self, which can lead to more stable and satisfying relationships.

While the process can be challenging and requires a significant commitment to introspection, the outcomes can be transformative, offering a pathway to lasting change and emotional resilience. For those struggling with the effects of anxious attachment, psychodynamic therapy provides a crucial platform for healing and growth.

COUPLES THERAPY

Couples therapy is a particularly effective approach to addressing anxious attachment within romantic relationships. This type of therapy facilitates a deeper understanding between partners and also fosters a secure attachment dynamic, which is crucial for those grappling with anxiety-driven attachment behaviors.

When tailored to address anxious attachment issues, couples therapy focuses on enhancing communication skills and emotional understanding between partners. It helps individuals express their needs and fears without triggering defensive responses from their partners. Therapists guide couples through exercises that promote empathy, allowing each partner to see the relationship from the other's perspective, which can be eye-opening and transformative.

One common technique used in this context is emotionally focused therapy (EFT), which delves into patterns in the relationship that contribute to insecurity and anxiety. Couples can create a more secure and supportive bond by identifying and addressing these patterns. EFT helps partners understand how their attachment styles influence their interactions and teaches them to respond in ways that reinforce trust and emotional safety.

Another aspect often explored in couples therapy is the role of individual histories. Understanding that early experiences shape one's attachment style can be enlightening for both partners. This awareness fosters patience and compassion as partners learn to react to each other's behaviors and understand the underlying vulnerabilities driving those behaviors.

Therapists often work with couples to establish new interaction patterns that promote security. This might involve setting routines that ensure time for emotional connection or creating 'rituals of connection' like daily debriefs or regular date nights, which can help mitigate feelings of neglect or abandonment experienced by those with anxious attachment styles.

The goal of couples therapy in the context of anxious attachment is not just to reduce symptoms of anxiety but to build a foundation of secure attachment from which both partners can grow. Through consistent and empathetic effort, couples can transform their relationship into a source of strength and stability, providing a secure base from which they can form closer connections.

GROUP THERAPY

Group therapy brings together people who share similar struggles, creating an environment where members can learn from each other's experiences and offer mutual support. The collective dynamic of a group setting helps demystify the feelings of isolation that often accompany anxious attachment. It can help individuals realize they are not alone in their feelings and behaviors.

In group therapy, individuals with anxious attachment can observe and reflect on the dynamics that unfold within the group, which can mirror their behaviors in relationships outside the therapy room. This mirroring can be incredibly enlightening. It allows participants to see firsthand how their attachment style influences their interactions and how they might perceive social cues differently from their peers.

One key benefit of group therapy is the opportunity to receive diverse feedback. For someone with an anxious attachment style, feedback from multiple perspectives can be instrumental in challenging their inherent assumptions about relationships and attachment. This feedback is not just from the therapist but also from peers who are facing similar issues. This can lead to a deeper understanding and sometimes a quicker reassessment of one's own behaviors and thought patterns.

I remember attending a group session where a young woman shared her fear of being too clingy in relationships. It struck a chord with me, as I had wrestled with similar fears in my own relationships. Hearing her story and the group's response helped me realize the commonality of our experiences and the possibilities for change. It was a moment of genuine connection and revelation for me and everyone in the room.

Group therapy also provides a safe space to practice new behaviors. For those with anxious attachment, it can be a place to experiment with expressing needs and boundaries without fear of rejection or judgment. Over time, this practice can enhance their relationship skills, increasing their confidence in interpersonal situations.

Group therapy offers a unique blend of support, insight, and practical learning that can be especially beneficial for those dealing with anxious attachment. It encourages community and understanding, fostering growth and healing in a shared, empathetic environment.

ONLINE THERAPY

In today's digital age, therapy accessibility has expanded significantly, thanks to the advent of online therapy options. For those grappling with anxious attachment, online therapy presents a particularly appealing avenue for several reasons. Firstly, it breaks down geographical barriers, allowing access to specialized therapists who might not be available locally. This is crucial for those living in remote areas or regions with a scarcity of mental health professionals.

Online therapy offers convenience and flexibility that traditional face-to-face sessions can't match. Sessions can be scheduled around personal and professional commitments, making it easier to maintain regular appointments—an essential aspect of effective therapy. This mode of therapy also tends to be less intimidating for many people, providing a sense of anonymity and privacy that can make individuals feel more comfortable sharing personal information.

Another significant advantage is the variety of communication modes available. Whether through video calls, messaging, or emails, online therapy can be tailored to the client's preferences, enhancing the therapeutic experience. This flexibility can be particularly beneficial for those with anxious attachment, who may find certain forms of communication less anxiety-provoking than others.

However, it's important to note that the lack of physical presence can sometimes make establishing a strong therapist-client relationship harder.

The benefits of online therapy often outweigh the drawbacks, especially for those dealing with anxious attachment. It provides an accessible, flexible, and less daunting way to understand and manage one's attachment style, ultimately leading to healthier relationships and improved overall well-being. As with any therapeutic approach, it's crucial to ensure that the online platform is secure and that the therapists are accredited, providing safe and professional services.

CHAPTER SUMMARY

- Cognitive Behavioral Therapy (CBT) helps individuals with anxious attachment by changing negative thought patterns and behaviors and improving relationship anxiety and attachment styles.
- Dialectical Behavior Therapy (DBT) is effective for emotional regulation and building interpersonal skills. It focuses on mindfulness, distress tolerance, emotion regulation, and interpersonal effectiveness.
- Psychodynamic therapy explores the deep-seated roots of emotional suffering from early relationships, enhancing self-awareness and

emotional insight for those with anxious attachment.
- Couples therapy addresses anxious attachment in relationships by enhancing communication, understanding attachment styles, and fostering secure attachment dynamics between partners.
- Group therapy provides a supportive environment for individuals with anxious attachment to learn from others' experiences, receive diverse feedback, and practice new behaviors.
- Online therapy offers accessibility, convenience, and a variety of communication modes. This makes it a suitable option for those with anxious attachment despite some challenges, like establishing a strong therapist-client relationship remotely.
- Each therapeutic approach offers unique benefits and strategies tailored to manage and improve anxious attachment issues.
- These therapies aim to foster healthier relationships, improve emotional regulation, and enhance overall well-being for individuals struggling with anxious attachment.

CHAPTER 6
SELF-HELP STRATEGIES

BUILDING SELF-ESTEEM

Building self-esteem can feel daunting, especially if you're grappling with an anxious attachment style. It often feels like a rollercoaster, where your self-worth might heavily affect how others perceive and treat you. But here's the good news: it's entirely possible to cultivate a stronger, more resilient sense of self.

First, let's talk about self-awareness. It's about understanding your thoughts, emotions, and behaviors. Recognizing patterns can help you see how your attachment style influences your self-esteem. For instance, you may notice that you seek validation excessively or adapt your behavior to please others, hoping to avoid rejection. Acknowledging these patterns is the first step towards change.

Now, onto self-compassion. This was a game-changer for me. I remember times when I'd beat myself up over a perceived slight or a social interaction that didn't go as planned. Learning to treat myself with the same kindness I'd extend to a good friend was transformative. It involves understanding that everyone has moments of doubt and that it's okay not to be perfect.

Engaging in activities reinforcing your sense of competence can bolster your self-esteem. Whether through professional achievements, creative endeavors, or physical activities, excelling in something you enjoy can significantly boost how you view yourself.

Lastly, consider therapy or counseling. Working with a professional can provide personalized strategies to build self-esteem and address your anxious attachment style. They can offer support and guidance tailored to your specific needs.

Building self-esteem is a journey, not a destination. It requires patience, persistence, and a lot of self-love. But with each step, you'll find yourself not only feeling better about who you are but also improving how you connect with others. It's about creating a healthier, happier you.

CREATING BOUNDARIES

Creating boundaries is a crucial step for individuals with anxious attachment styles. It can help foster healthier relationships and improve self-esteem. When you have an anxious attachment style, you might find yourself overly concerned about the opinions and actions of others, often leading to a blurred line between personal needs and the desires of those around you. Establishing clear boundaries is not about pushing others away but setting a comfortable space where mutual respect and understanding can thrive.

Firstly, it's important to understand what boundaries are. Boundaries are the limits you set for yourself and others, defining what you find acceptable and unacceptable behavior from those around you. Boundaries can be emotional, physical, or even digital in today's connected world. For example, deciding not to answer work calls after a particular hour sets a boundary that helps you manage work-life balance.

To start creating boundaries, you need to do some introspection. Identify areas where you feel discomfort, resentment, or energy loss in your relationships. These feelings often signal where boundaries need to be established. For instance, if you feel drained after interactions with a particular friend who often vents to you, it might be time to limit how often you engage in emotionally heavy conversations.

Communicating your boundaries clearly and assertively is next. This doesn't mean being aggressive or confrontational. It's about being honest and direct about your needs. You might say, "I care about you and our conversations, but I need to limit the time I can spend discussing stressful topics." It's crucial to stick to your boundaries once they are communicated. People might test them, not out of disrespect, but to understand the limits—consistency in your responses reinforces your boundaries.

When you have an anxious attachment style, setting boundaries can initially feel daunting because you fear rejection or abandonment. However, it's important to remember that healthy boundaries are not about creating distance but about fostering genuine connections based on mutual respect. It might feel uncomfortable initially, especially if you're not used to asserting your needs.

Start small by setting minor boundaries in less emotionally charged situations. This could be as simple as deciding not to respond to non-urgent messages immediately or taking a few minutes each day to decompress. These small steps can build confidence and demonstrate that boundaries do not lead to negative outcomes but enhance your well-being and relationships. With practice, it becomes more natural, and your relationships will likely improve. Those who care for you will respect your boundaries and adjust their interactions accordingly.

Be prepared to reassess and adjust your boundaries as needed. Life changes, and so do relationships and personal needs. Regularly reflecting on and adjusting your boundaries is a healthy practice that can help you maintain good emotional health and relationship satisfaction.

By mastering the art of setting and maintaining boundaries, you empower yourself to build stronger, more meaningful connections with others while protecting your mental health and well-being.

EMOTIONAL REGULATION TECHNIQUES

When dealing with anxious attachment, emotions can often feel like a wild roller coaster—unpredictable, intense, and sometimes overwhelming. Learning to regulate these emotions benefits your well-being and mental health. Emotional regulation doesn't mean suppressing your feelings. It's about understanding, processing, and responding to your emotions in a healthy and productive way.

Deep Breathing

One effective technique is deep breathing. It sounds simple, and it is, but its impact should not be underestimated. When you start to feel anxiety building, take a moment to focus solely on your breathing. Inhale slowly through your nose, hold for a few seconds and exhale through your mouth. Repeat this several times. This method helps reduce the immediate physiological responses to stress, such as a racing heart or quickened breathing.

Mindfulness and Meditation

Mindfulness and meditation are powerful tools for managing the anxiety and preoccupation often experienced by individuals with anxious attachment styles. These practices foster a greater awareness of the present moment and reduce the tendency to ruminate on past interactions or worry about future relationships.

Mindfulness involves paying attention to the present moment without judgment. For someone with an anxious attachment, this means observing thoughts and feelings related to attachment anxieties as they arise, acknowledging them, and letting them pass without criticism. This can be particularly helpful during moments of heightened anxiety, where the mind might typically spiral into worst-case scenarios.

Meditation, on the other hand, can cultivate a deeper sense of calm and inner peace, which can counteract feelings of insecurity and neediness. Techniques like focused attention meditation, where you concentrate on a single point of reference, such as your breath, can enhance your ability to concentrate and stay centered amidst emotional turmoil.

Over time, regular meditation practice can help alter the habitual responses that characterize anxious attachment, leading to more balanced emotional reactions and healthier relationship dynamics.

When practicing mindfulness or meditation for the first time, it's beneficial to start small—perhaps with a daily five-minute session—and gradually increase the duration as comfort with the practice grows. Numerous apps and online resources are available to guide beginners through the basics of these practices.

Integrating mindfulness and meditation into your daily routine can improve your management of anxious attachment by enhancing emotional regulation and developing a greater sense of personal stability. This, in turn, can lead to more secure and satisfying relationships. Apps and guided meditations can be a good starting point if you're new to mindfulness.

Cognitive Restructuring

Lastly, cognitive restructuring, often used in cognitive-behavioral therapy, involves challenging and changing distressing thoughts. Anxious attachments can generate many "what if" scenarios, leading to unnecessary distress. You can significantly reduce emotional distress by examining these thoughts critically and replacing them with more balanced ones.

These techniques are not just coping mechanisms but stepping stones to a more secure and stable emotional life. Practice them regularly, and you might find that not only do your relationships improve, but your overall mental well-being does, too. Remember, the goal isn't to eliminate anxiety but to manage it so that it no longer controls your life.

JOURNALING

Journaling can be a powerful tool for gaining emotional clarity. This simple practice helps you untangle the web of thoughts and feelings often accompanying an anxious attachment style, providing a clearer path forward.

When you have an anxious attachment style, you might be overwhelmed by worries about your relationships. You may fear being abandoned or constantly seek reassurance from others. Journaling offers a private space to express these fears without judgment, allowing you to process your emotions at your own pace.

Start by setting aside a few minutes each day to write. You don't need anything fancy—just a notebook and a pen or a digital device if you prefer typing. The key is consistency. Make this a daily ritual, perhaps every morning, to set the tone for the day or every evening to reflect on the day's events.

In your journal, focus on your feelings and why you think you're feeling it. For instance, if you felt anxious after a friend or partner didn't return your text quickly, write about that experience. Explore the thoughts that raced through your mind and how it impacted your mood. This process helps you identify patterns in your thoughts and behaviors, making them easier to address.

Another helpful technique is to write letters in your journal that you don't intend to send. These could be to a specific person who triggers your anxious attachment or even to yourself. Express everything you wish you could say. This can be a therapeutic way to release emotions you might be holding back in your interactions.

Journaling also allows you to track your progress over time. As you read past entries, you likely notice changes in how you handle similar situations. This can be incredibly encouraging and motivate you to continue using journaling as a tool for emotional growth.

The goal of journaling isn't to have perfect grammar or to write dramatic statements—it's about honest self-expression. Let your thoughts flow freely, and don't worry about how it sounds. This is just for you, a safe space to confront and comfort your inner self, helping you navigate the complexities of anxious attachment with greater ease and understanding.

CHAPTER SUMMARY

- Building self-esteem involves recognizing and changing patterns influenced by anxious attachment, such as seeking excessive validation or adapting behavior to avoid rejection.
- Self-compassion, setting personal boundaries, and engaging in competence-reinforcing activities are helpful strategies for enhancing self-esteem.

- Creating boundaries involves defining acceptable behaviors and limits in relationships, which helps improve self-esteem and relationship dynamics.
- Emotional regulation techniques like deep breathing, meditation, and mindfulness help manage the intense emotions associated with anxious attachment.
- Mindfulness and meditation help manage anxiety by increasing present-moment awareness and reducing rumination. This can be beneficial for those with anxious attachment styles.
- Starting with short, daily sessions of mindfulness or meditation can help build a routine. Many apps and resources are available to guide you.
- Journaling provides a private space to express fears and anxieties, helping to identify patterns and track emotional growth over time.

CHAPTER 7
NAVIGATING RELATIONSHIPS

Navigating relationships when you have an anxious attachment style can feel like you're constantly walking a tightrope. Imagine, for a moment, that every interaction with a loved one is filtered through a lens of worry about their affection and fear of losing them. This can make maintaining healthy, balanced relationships quite challenging.

For those with anxious attachment, there's often an increased sensitivity to the emotional tone of interactions. A simple unanswered text message or a change in plans can spiral into anxiety and fear of abandonment. It's like having an internal alarm system that is too sensitive, ringing loud warnings at the slightest hint of distance or disapproval.

Communication is key to managing these feelings. It's important to express your needs and fears openly to your partners or friends and listen to their needs and boundaries. This two-way street of communication helps build a foundation of understanding and trust.

It's equally important to work on self-awareness. Recognizing the triggers that set off your anxious reactions can help you to pause and assess whether your fears are based on the current reality or past insecurities. This awareness can be slow and often challenging but is crucial for growth.

Building self-reliance is another vital step. While seeking reassurance from others is natural, finding confidence in your own worth independently of your relationships can provide a more stable emotional base. This might involve engaging in activities that boost your self-esteem, seeking therapy, or practicing mindfulness and meditation.

Lastly, remember the importance of setting and respecting boundaries. This might mean learning to give your partner space without feeling abandoned or communicating your need for space without guilt. Boundaries help define the limits of your comfort zone in relationships, and respecting them can prevent feelings of resentment or anxiety from building up.

Navigating relationships with an anxious attachment style isn't easy, but with the right tools and support, it's possible to build lasting, healthy connections. Remember, the goal isn't to change who you are but to understand and manage how you connect with others. This journey towards secure attachment is about improving your relationships and enriching your emotional landscape.

ATTACHMENT STYLES IN PARTNERS

Understanding how different attachment styles interact in relationships can be quite an eye-opener. For instance, when someone with an anxious attachment style partners with someone who has a secure attachment style, the dynamics can either be harmonious or challenging, depending on various factors.

Anxiously attached individuals often seek constant reassurance and closeness, which can feel overwhelming to their partners if not understood properly. Partners with a secure attachment style can provide the stability and reassurance that anxious individuals crave, potentially leading to a balanced relationship.

Conversely, a relationship between an anxiously attached individual and an avoidantly attached partner can be tumultuous. The anxious partner's need for closeness can clash with the avoidant's need for independence, leading to a cycle of push and pull that can be emotionally draining for both parties.

I've seen this dynamic play out among friends and family. A close friend of mine, who identifies with having an anxious attachment style, found herself constantly unsettled by her partner's avoidant tendencies. It was a classic case of her needing more closeness than her partner was comfortable giving. Over time, with lots of communication and some counseling, they have started better understanding each other's needs, working towards a more secure relationship dynamic.

Understanding and respecting each other's attachment styles can lead to healthier interactions and a deeper connection in any relationship. It's about finding balance, communicating openly, and seeking external help when needed to bridge the gap between different attachment needs.

COMMUNICATION PATTERNS

Communication patterns often manifest uniquely in relationships, influencing both the dynamics of a relationship and the emotional well-being of the individuals involved.

Someone with anxious attachment often has a heightened need for assurance, leading to a communication style characterized by frequent requests for confirmation of affection and commitment. For example, they might frequently ask their partner if they are truly loved or happy in the relationship. While these questions stem from a place of genuine need, they can sometimes overwhelm their partner, potentially leading to tension or misunderstandings.

Those with anxious attachment might interpret ambiguous statements or behaviors from their partners as negative or threatening, even when no harm is intended. This can lead to what is often called 'reading between the lines' excessively, where they might overanalyze texts, facial expressions, or offhand remarks, usually assuming the worst. Consequently, this often results in emotional volatility within relationships, where periods of intense closeness are interspersed with episodes of conflict or distress.

Communication for those with anxious attachment can also be paradoxical. On the one hand, they want to express their feelings and fears openly to alleviate their anxiety. On the other hand, they might hold back from communicating openly due to the fear of rejection or being seen as needy. This internal conflict can prevent the establishment of a stable, open line of communication, which is essential for healthy relationships.

It's crucial for individuals with anxious attachment to work on self-awareness and emotional regulation to foster healthier communication patterns. Recognizing the triggers that lead to insecurity and learning to communicate these feelings constructively can help reduce misunderstandings. Therapy and self-help strategies, such as those mentioned in the previous chapter, can be invaluable tools in this journey.

Understanding and patience are key for partners of those with an anxious attachment style. Consistent and clear communication, as well as reassuring love and commitment, can help build a secure foundation for the relationship. It's about finding a balance where both partners feel heard and valued without one having to constantly soothe the other's fears.

While anxious attachment can complicate communication patterns, recognizing and addressing these issues opens the door to more meaningful and resilient relationships. Through mutual understanding and effort, both partners can navigate the complexities of attachment and communication, leading to a stronger, healthier bond.

REBUILDING TRUST

Rebuilding trust in relationships, especially when dealing with anxious attachment, can feel like navigating a labyrinth —complex and fraught with unexpected turns. For those with an anxious attachment style, trust is not just a part of the relationship; it's the cornerstone that can often feel shaky or insufficiently anchored.

Imagine, for a moment, a situation where a simple

misunderstanding led to a week of uneasy texts and sleepless nights. This isn't just a common scenario—it's a lived reality for many grappling with anxious attachment. The fear that loved ones will leave or become disinterested can cloud judgment, turning even minor issues into potential relationship-enders.

Rebuilding trust starts with open communication. This means expressing fears and insecurities without the expectation of immediate resolution. It's about creating a dialogue where both parties feel heard and valued. For instance, instead of accusing a partner of spending too little time with you, explain how their actions make you feel and discuss ways to spend quality time together that reassure both of you.

Another key element is consistency. Small, consistent actions over time, like regular check-ins or affirmations, can significantly strengthen the trust foundation. It's not about grand gestures but rather the daily reassurances and reliable behaviors that build security and demonstrate commitment.

Patience plays a pivotal role as well. Rebuilding trust doesn't happen overnight. It requires time, during which both partners must actively commit to understanding and adapting to each other's attachment needs. This might mean working through misunderstandings without jumping to conclusions or withdrawing emotionally at the first sign of conflict.

Therapeutic interventions can also be beneficial. Couples or individual therapy can provide tools and strategies to manage anxious behaviors and foster a healthier, more secure relational dynamic. Therapists can help identify underlying issues that fuel attachment fears and guide couples through exercises that build trust and intimacy.

Lastly, it's important to celebrate small victories. Every step forward, no matter how minor it seems, is progress. Acknowledging and appreciating these moments can motivate both partners to continue working on the relationship.

Rebuilding trust with an anxious attachment style isn't just about managing fears—it's about transforming them into opportunities for growth and deeper connection. With the right approach, patience, and understanding, the labyrinth of trust becomes less daunting, leading to a path where secure, fulfilling relationships can flourish.

HANDLING CONFLICTS

Individuals with anxious attachment often face unique challenges when handling conflicts. Their inherent fear of abandonment and rejection can make every disagreement feel like a potential threat to the relationship. This heightened sensitivity to conflict can lead to behaviors that either escalate the situation or avoid it entirely, neither of which is particularly healthy or constructive.

Firstly, those with anxious attachment need to recognize their patterns in conflict situations. Typically, they might respond with a flood of emotions and a sense of urgency to resolve the issue immediately. This can overwhelm their partner, who might need more time to process the situation. On the flip side, fearing the worst, they might withdraw completely, hoping to avoid confrontation but instead creating a distance that wasn't there before.

For those with anxious attachment, expressing feelings without accusations or dramatics is essential. Simple, clear statements about how a situation makes them feel can be more effective than an emotionally charged accusation. For example, saying, "I feel worried when you don't call me at the agreed time," directly addresses the concern without blaming the other person.

Listening is just as essential as speaking. Partners of those with anxious attachment should strive to be patient and reassuring without being dismissive. Acknowledging the feelings expressed without necessarily agreeing with every point helps validate the concerns of an anxiously attached individual, which can be soothing.

Setting boundaries around conflict can also be beneficial. This might mean agreeing not to discuss serious topics late at night or setting a time limit on discussions to prevent exhaustion and resentment. It's about finding a balance that respects both partners' emotional states.

It's also beneficial for those with anxious attachment to work on self-soothing techniques. Practices like deep breathing, mindfulness, or even stepping away for a moment can help manage the intense emotions that arise during conflicts. This not only aids in handling the immediate situation more calmly but also contributes to long-term emotional regulation skills.

Handling conflicts for someone with anxious attachment doesn't mean changing who they are but instead adapting how they react to and process conflicts. Conflicts can be navigated more smoothly with awareness, communication, and some strategy.

MAINTAINING INDEPENDENCE

Maintaining independence in relationships can often feel like navigating a minefield for individuals with an anxious attachment style . The fear of being too distant can be just as paralyzing as being too clingy. However, fostering a sense of independence is not only possible but essential for healthy, balanced relationships.

It's essential to understand that independence in a relationship doesn't mean emotional detachment or physical distance. Instead, it's about having a secure sense of self and enjoying activities and interests outside the relationship without excessive anxiety. This can be challenging for those with anxious attachment, as their self-worth may heavily depend on their partner's mood and actions.

One effective strategy is to develop hobbies and interests separate from your partner's. This not only helps in building self-esteem but also provides a healthy outlet for stress and anxiety. Whether painting, hiking, reading, or any other activity, the key is to engage in it because it brings you joy and fulfillment, not because you're trying to escape from relationship anxieties.

Communication is also essential in maintaining independence. It's important to discuss your needs and boundaries with your partner openly. This might include setting aside time for yourself or explaining why certain activities are essential to your growth. Remember, expressing your needs doesn't mean pushing your partner away. On the contrary, it can deepen understanding and intimacy.

While maintaining independence in relationships can be

particularly challenging for those with anxious attachment styles, it is deeply rewarding. It leads to healthier relationships and a stronger, more resilient sense of self. Remember, independence and intimacy are not mutually exclusive but are, in fact, complementary components of a loving relationship.

CHAPTER SUMMARY

- Individuals with anxious attachment styles often experience heightened sensitivity in relationships, fearing abandonment and constantly seeking reassurance.
- Effective communication is crucial for managing anxious attachment.
- Self-awareness and building self-reliance help individuals with anxious attachment styles to stabilize their emotions and improve relationships.
- Setting and respecting boundaries is essential to prevent resentment and manage anxiety in relationships.
- Anxious attachment can lead to challenging dynamics, especially when paired with avoidant attachment styles, but can be balanced with secure partners.
- Communication patterns for those with anxious attachment often involve needing frequent reassurance, which can strain relationships.

- Rebuilding trust in relationships with anxious attachment involves open communication, consistency, and therapeutic interventions.
- Maintaining independence in relationships is vital for those with anxious attachment. It involves setting personal boundaries and developing individual interests.

CHAPTER 8
SUPPORT AND RESOURCES

FINDING THE RIGHT THERAPIST

Finding the right therapist can be a game-changer when managing anxious attachment. Though deeply personal, this journey doesn't have to be daunting. Here's some guidance to help you navigate this important step.

Firstly, consider the type of therapy that might suit your needs. Since anxious attachment often involves fear of abandonment and issues with self-esteem, therapies like Cognitive Behavioral Therapy (CBT) or Psychodynamic Therapy are often recommended. These therapies focus on understanding and changing thought patterns or exploring past experiences that might influence your current state.

Next, look for a therapist who specializes in attachment issues. Therapists with this focus will have a deeper understanding of the dynamics of anxious attachment and can provide targeted strategies to manage it. You can start your search through online directories or local mental health organizations. Don't hesitate to ask potential therapists about their experience with attachment theory and their approach to treating it.

It's also important to consider the logistics. Decide whether you prefer face-to-face sessions or if online therapy suits your lifestyle better. Online therapy has become a viable option, offering flexibility and accessibility, especially if finding time or commuting is challenging.

Once you have a shortlist, reach out and arrange initial consultations. Many therapists offer a brief initial session free of charge, which can be an excellent opportunity to see if you feel comfortable with their style and approach. During these sessions, ask about their treatment methods, experience with anxious attachment, and any other concerns you might have.

Remember, your relationship with your therapist is crucial. You need to feel safe, understood, and respected. Trust your gut feeling during these initial interactions. If something doesn't feel right, it's perfectly okay to look for another therapist. There's no one-size-fits-all, and finding the right match can sometimes take a few tries.

Lastly, give yourself credit for taking this step. Seeking help is a sign of strength, not weakness. With the right support, you can understand your attachment style better and develop healthier relationships. Remember that therapy is a journey, often with ups and downs, but finding the right therapist can make all the difference in navigating this path successfully.

SUPPORT GROUPS AND COMMUNITIES

Navigating the world with an anxious attachment style can often feel like sailing in stormy seas. The good news? You're not alone, and there are communities and support groups that can offer you a safe harbor. These groups provide a space to share your experiences, learn from others, and gain the support you need to manage or transform your attachment style.

Support groups for those with anxious attachment often focus on building a sense of community and trust among members. This is crucial because trust can be a significant issue for individuals with anxious attachment. In these groups, you'll find people who understand your unique challenges, such as fear of abandonment, difficulty trusting partners, or the tendency to cling to relationships.

These communities can be found in various formats. Some are formal, therapist-led groups that meet regularly in person or online. These groups often combine sharing sessions with structured therapeutic activities to help members understand their attachment style and develop healthier relationship skills.

Online forums and social media groups offer another layer of support. These platforms provide continuous access to a community where you can share successes and setbacks as they happen. The real-time feedback and encouragement can be incredibly reassuring, especially during moments of anxiety or doubt.

Local community centers and mental health clinics often host support groups. Participating in a local group has the added benefit of meeting people in your area, which can lead to friendships and a support network outside of group meetings.

Choose a support group that feels right for you. Some groups focus more on discussion, while others incorporate more therapeutic exercises. The key is to find a group where you feel safe and supported.

Remember, the goal of joining these groups isn't just to find support and learn and practice new ways of forming and maintaining secure relationships. Over time, these interactions can help you develop a more secure attachment style, leading to healthier and more rewarding relationships.

If you're struggling with anxious attachment, consider reaching out to a support group. It could be the first step toward a more stable and satisfying relational world. Whether online or in person, these communities can offer invaluable support, insights, and the chance to connect with others who truly understand what you're going through.

BOOKS AND ONLINE RESOURCES

Diving into the world of literature on anxious attachment can be incredibly helpful for anyone looking to understand more about this attachment style, whether for personal insight or to support someone else. There's a wealth of resources out there that can help deepen your understanding and provide practical advice for managing anxious attachment in various aspects of life.

The internet is a treasure trove of resources for those dealing with anxious attachment. Whether you seek understanding, guidance, or community support, numerous websites, forums, and online tools are available.

Websites like Psychology Today offer comprehensive articles that delve into the nuances of anxious attachment, helping you understand its origins and manifestations. These resources are invaluable for those just beginning to explore the implications of their attachment style on their relationships and personal well-being.

For those seeking more interactive support, online forums such as Reddit and Quora provide platforms where individuals can share their experiences and advice. Here, you can find communities specifically focused on attachment issues, where members actively discuss their struggles and triumphs in overcoming the challenges associated with anxious attachment.

Several mental health platforms offer online therapy services that cater specifically to attachment-related issues. Websites like BetterHelp and Talkspace allow you to connect with therapists who specialize in attachment theory and can provide personalized guidance and support through secure, convenient online sessions.

Lastly, educational websites like The Attachment Project offer courses and workshops focusing on understanding and healing from different attachment styles. These resources can be beneficial for those who want to take a deep dive into personal development and recovery.

By leveraging books and online resources, you can gain insights, find support, and access tools that facilitate personal growth and healthier relationships. Whether reading informative articles, participating in community discussions, engaging in therapy, or using self-help apps, the path to understanding and managing anxious attachment is more accessible than ever.

APPS AND TOOLS

In today's digital age, a variety of apps and tools can help manage anxious attachment. These resources offer practical support at your fingertips, often blending technology with traditional therapeutic techniques to provide users with accessible and practical solutions.

One popular category of apps focuses on mindfulness and meditation, which can be particularly beneficial for those dealing with anxious attachment. Apps like Headspace and Calm offer guided meditation sessions that help users reduce anxiety, increase awareness of their emotional states, and develop a deeper sense of calm. By regularly practicing mindfulness, individuals can learn to respond to stressors more effectively rather than reacting impulsively due to their attachment anxieties.

Another helpful tool is mood-tracking apps such as Daylio or MoodNotes. These apps allow users to track their emotional states over time, helping them identify triggers and patterns in their feelings and behaviors. Understanding these patterns can be crucial in managing anxious attachment, as it empowers individuals to anticipate and prepare for situations that might challenge their emotional equilibrium.

Additionally, some apps are designed to address the dynamics of personal relationships, which can be particularly strained by anxious attachment. Apps like Lasting or Relish offer relationship counseling and exercises couples can do together to strengthen their bond and improve communication. These tools can be instrumental in helping individuals with anxious attachment build healthier, more secure relationships.

For those who prefer a self-help approach, apps like What's Up? utilize Cognitive Behavioral Therapy (CBT) techniques to help users challenge distorted thinking and change behavioral patterns. By providing exercises focusing on cognitive restructuring and behavioral modification, these apps can help individuals with anxious attachment develop healthier ways of thinking and reacting to their anxieties.

Incorporating these apps and tools can enhance your ability to manage anxious attachment. They provide practical, accessible, and often immediate support to help you navigate the challenges of this attachment style, ultimately leading to improved mental health and more robust, more resilient relationships.

EMERGENCY ASSISTANCE

When dealing with anxious attachment, moments may arise that feel overwhelming, pushing you toward a state of crisis. It's crucial to recognize when you're reaching a breaking point and know that emergency assistance is available to help you navigate these intense periods.

Firstly, if you find yourself in a severe emotional crisis, consider reaching out to a mental health hotline. These hotlines are staffed with trained professionals who offer immediate support and can guide you to further resources, such as local mental health services or crisis centers. Remember, these services are confidential and often available 24/7, ensuring you have support whenever needed.

Another vital resource is the emergency room at your

local hospital. If you're experiencing extreme distress or have thoughts of self-harm, the emergency room can provide immediate intervention and ensure your safety. The healthcare professionals there can also help connect you with long-term mental health support following the crisis.

For those who might find themselves in less immediate but still urgent emotional distress, scheduling an emergency session with their therapist can be a beneficial step. Many therapists offer crisis slots for their clients, understanding that sometimes the need for help can't wait until the next scheduled appointment.

Lastly, don't underestimate the power of your personal support network. Friends, family, or members of support groups specifically for those with anxious attachment can provide emotional support and practical help during a crisis. Sometimes, talking things through with someone who understands can be incredibly soothing and grounding.

Recognizing when you need emergency assistance is a sign of strength and self-awareness, not a weakness. By knowing what resources are available and how to access them, you empower yourself to manage your attachment style proactively and healthily.

CHAPTER SUMMARY

- When managing anxious attachment, it is beneficial to find a therapist who specializes in attachment issues and therapies like CBT or Psychodynamic Therapy.

- Consider logistics like preferring online or face-to-face therapy sessions and arrange initial consultations to gauge comfort and fit with the therapist.
- Trust your instincts about the therapeutic relationship; feeling safe and respected is crucial, and it's okay to try different therapists.
- Support groups and communities offer a space to share experiences and learn from others with similar challenges, helping to build trust and understanding.
- Books and online resources, including websites like Psychology Today, offer articles, community support, and access to therapists specializing in attachment issues.
- Apps like Headspace and Calm for mindfulness and Talkspace or BetterHelp for teletherapy support managing anxious attachment through technology.
- In emergencies, utilize mental health hotlines, emergency rooms, or digital crisis management tools, and don't hesitate to rely on your personal support networks.

CHAPTER 9
PERSONAL GROWTH AND DEVELOPMENT

SETTING PERSONAL GOALS

Setting goals is a fundamental step for personal growth, especially for individuals grappling with anxious attachment. Goals provide direction and measurable milestones that can boost your self-esteem and sense of accomplishment as you progress. However, for those with anxious attachment, the process of setting and pursuing goals can be intertwined with fears of failure or rejection. Here, we'll explore practical strategies to set personal goals that are both ambitious and attainable while also being mindful of the unique challenges posed by anxious attachment.

Firstly, it's crucial to understand the importance of setting realistic goals. While it's great to aim high, overly ambitious goals can sometimes set you up for disappointment. Start small. For instance, if your ultimate goal is to enhance your relationships, begin by setting a goal to communicate more openly with your friends or partner about your needs and feelings. This step-by-step approach makes the goal more manageable and less daunting.

Secondly, embrace flexibility in your goal-setting. Life is unpredictable, and being too rigid in your goals can lead to frustration and self-criticism. Allow yourself the space to adjust your goals as needed. This adaptability can help reduce anxiety about achieving perfection or meeting strict timelines, which often accompany anxious attachment.

Thirdly, focus on process-oriented goals instead of outcome-oriented ones. For example, instead of setting a goal to 'make three new friends,' which focuses on an outcome that's not entirely within your control, set a goal to 'attend two social events per month.' This shift in focus helps you concentrate on actions you can control, reducing anxiety and building confidence in social settings.

It's helpful to practice self-compassion throughout your goal-setting journey. Remember, progress is not linear, and setbacks are part of the process. You might be harsh on yourself for not meeting expectations quickly enough. Acknowledging your efforts and celebrating small victories along the way is essential. This practice can reinforce a positive self-view and encourage persistence.

Remember to seek support when you need it. Sharing your goals with a therapist, a coach, or even a trusted friend can provide you with encouragement and accountability. Having reassurance from others can be comforting and diminish feelings of isolation or fear of failure.

LEARNING NEW SKILLS

Learning new skills can be an incredibly transformative experience. This process fosters personal growth and provides a practical framework for enhancing self-esteem and autonomy—key areas often compromised by an anxious attachment style.

The fear of failure or rejection can be paralyzing when approaching new learning opportunities. However, embracing a mindset of growth and resilience can shift this perspective. Start small; choose a skill that interests you but doesn't overwhelm you. Whether it's cooking, photography, coding, or even gardening, the key is to do something that feels manageable and enjoyable.

Structured learning environments can also be particularly beneficial. Consider enrolling in a class or workshop where regular sessions can provide the necessary discipline and a sense of progress. These settings also offer the added benefit of social interaction, which can help ease the feelings of isolation often associated with anxious attachment.

It's also important to reflect on your learning journey. Keep a journal or blog about what you're learning, the challenges you face, and the successes you achieve. This reflection not only consolidates your learning but also builds self-awareness.

EMBRACING CHANGE

Change, especially significant life changes, can be a daunting prospect for anyone, but it poses a unique set of challenges for those with an anxious attachment style. Embracing change involves stepping into the unknown, a scenario that typically triggers anxiety and fear in individuals who crave certainty and security.

For someone with an anxious attachment style, the mere thought of change can evoke intense feelings of insecurity and apprehension. This is because their attachment system is calibrated to be highly sensitive to threats to closeness and security. However, change is an inevitable part of life and personal growth. Learning to navigate and embrace it is not just beneficial; it's necessary.

The first step in embracing change is understanding and acknowledging your fears. It's okay to feel scared or worried about what lies ahead. These feelings are valid and quite common. However, dwelling on them without taking action can lead to stagnation. Instead, try to articulate what exactly about the change feels threatening. Is it the fear of losing someone? The uncertainty of a new job? Or the discomfort of stepping out of your comfort zone? Identifying your fear's root cause can help address it more effectively.

Next, it's crucial to build a support system. This doesn't mean you need a vast network of friends or family. Even one or two close relationships where you feel secure and supported can make a significant difference. These relationships provide a safe base from which you can explore new aspects of life and return to when you feel overwhelmed.

It's okay to seek professional help. Therapy can be incredibly beneficial in understanding and modifying anxious attachment behaviors. A therapist can provide strategies tailored to your needs, helping you navigate changes more smoothly.

Embracing change is not about eliminating fear but about

moving forward despite it. It's about understanding that the security you seek can be carried within yourself through self-assurance, resilience, and supportive relationships. Change is about facing the new and letting go of old patterns that no longer serve you. It's a rewarding journey toward personal growth and development, allowing you to become more resilient and confident.

YOUR SELF-DISCOVERY JOURNEY

Self-discovery involves uncovering deeper insights about yourself and learning how to manage and reshape the anxieties that often come with your attachment style. It's about turning inward, reflecting, and gradually stepping out of the comfort zones dictated by past attachment experiences.

For someone with an anxious attachment style, self-discovery often starts with recognizing how their fears of abandonment and need for closeness affect their behavior and relationships. It's a moment of realization that these patterns, although deeply ingrained, are not fixed traits but aspects of oneself that can be understood and modified.

The journey includes exploring past experiences that contributed to the development of anxious attachment. This might involve revisiting childhood memories or past relationships, not dwelling on them but understanding their impact. The goal here is not to assign blame but to clarify how these experiences have shaped one's relationship expectations and reactions.

A crucial part of this journey is learning to nurture a compassionate relationship with yourself. This means practicing self-compassion and kindness, especially in moments of self-doubt or when you feel clingy or overly dependent. It's about affirming that it's okay to need others and reinforcing the importance of self-reliance and personal strength.

Journaling serves as a reflective practice that can enhance self-discovery. It provides a private space to express emotions and thoughts, which is therapeutic for those who may not have had their feelings validated. Through regular journaling, you can start to identify triggers and patterns in your behavior, making it easier to address them constructively.

The self-discovery journey for someone with an anxious attachment style involves moving from a place of fear and dependency to one of understanding and self-assurance. It's a transformative process that improves relationships with others and fundamentally changes how one views and treats oneself.

CELEBRATING SUCCESSES

As we journey through understanding and managing anxious attachment, we must pause and recognize the milestones achieved along the way. Celebrating successes is vital in personal growth and development, no matter how small they seem.

When dealing with anxious attachment, progress can often feel slow and sometimes invisible. It's easy to overlook the small victories—like setting a boundary, expressing your needs clearly, or even recognizing when you're spiraling into anxiety. However, acknowledging these moments can reinforce your self-worth and motivate you to continue working on your attachment issues.

Celebration doesn't always mean throwing a party or making a grand gesture. It can be as simple as taking a moment to yourself to reflect on what you've accomplished. Perhaps you journal about it, share your progress with a supportive friend or therapist, or treat yourself to something you enjoy. Celebrating helps cement the positive changes you're making and can shift your focus from what's going wrong to what's going right.

Recognizing your own progress is incredibly empowering. It's a way to see that you are capable of change and that your efforts are bearing fruit. This can be incredibly reassuring and diminish the insecurity often accompanying anxious attachment.

Incorporating celebration into your life might also involve setting regular intervals to review your progress. It could be once a month or at the end of every therapy session. Use these times to reflect on what you've learned and how you've grown. This enhances your appreciation for the journey and helps you set clear goals for the future.

Remember, every step forward is a step away from the grip of anxious attachment and towards a more happy, loving life. Let each success, no matter how small, be a stepping stone and a reason for celebration. This approach enriches your journey and transforms the recovery process into a series of achievements worth celebrating.

CHAPTER SUMMARY

- Setting goals is crucial for personal growth, especially for those with anxious attachment, providing direction and measurable milestones.
- Start with realistic and manageable goals, like improving communication in relationships, and allow flexibility to adjust goals as needed. Focus on process-oriented goals that are within your control, such as attending social events, rather than outcome-oriented goals.
- Practice self-compassion throughout goal-setting, acknowledging your efforts, and celebrating small victories to boost self-esteem.
- Seek support from therapists, coaches, or friends to provide encouragement and accountability, which is comforting for those with anxious attachment.
- Learning new skills can enhance self-esteem and autonomy, with structured learning environments providing discipline and social interaction.
- Embrace change by understanding and acknowledging fears, building a support system, and developing resilience through small, achievable goals.
- Celebrate successes, no matter how small, to reinforce self-worth and motivate continued progress on managing anxious attachment.

CHAPTER 10
CASE STUDIES AND REAL-LIFE EXAMPLES

The following case studies illustrate the effectiveness of various therapeutic approaches, including individual therapy, couples therapy, group therapy, and self-help strategies, in managing and overcoming anxious attachment.

They highlight the importance of personalized therapeutic interventions, the transformative potential of therapy, and the value of persistence and support in achieving healthier, more secure relational patterns.

CASE STUDY 1: INDIVIDUAL THERAPY

In our first case study, we explore the journey of Emma, a 35-year-old marketing executive who sought individual therapy to address her anxious attachment issues, which she felt were undermining her relationships and self-esteem.

Emma's therapy began with her describing a pattern of feeling overly dependent on the emotional availability of her partners. She often found herself in a state of constant anxiety, fearing rejection and abandonment. This fear was not only exhausting but also strained her relationships, leading to a vicious cycle of clinginess followed by inevitable breakdowns.

Her therapist used a combination of cognitive-behavioral therapy techniques to help Emma identify and challenge her beliefs about her self-worth and the security of her relationships. Through sessions focused on understanding the roots of her anxiety, Emma learned that her attachment style was primarily influenced by her childhood experiences with her caregivers, who often left her alone and were emotionally unavailable at times of need.

One breakthrough moment came when Emma was able to connect her adult fears of abandonment with specific childhood incidents. This insight was pivotal; it allowed her to view her current anxieties through a more compassionate lens, understanding them as learned responses rather than inherent flaws.

Emma also worked on developing healthier communication patterns as part of her therapy. She practiced expressing her needs and desires in relationships without the overwhelming fear of negative outcomes. Her therapist introduced role-playing exercises, which were initially challenging but gradually helped her gain confidence in handling interpersonal conflicts more assertively.

After several months of consistent therapy, Emma noticed a significant improvement in her relationships. She felt more secure and confident and was better equipped to foster healthy attachments. Her story is a testament to the transformative power of individual therapy tailored to address the specific challenges of anxious attachment.

Emma's case highlights the importance of personalized therapeutic interventions in managing anxious attachment and illustrates how therapy can empower individuals to rewrite their attachment narratives toward better, more secure relationships.

CASE STUDY 2: COUPLES THERAPY

In this case study, we explore the journey of Emily and Mark, a couple who sought therapy to address the challenges stemming from Emily's anxious attachment style. Emily, often feeling insecure about Mark's commitment, sought constant reassurance from him, which led to frequent misunderstandings and arguments.

The couple decided to engage in couples therapy after a particularly intense disagreement that made them question the viability of their relationship. During their sessions, the therapist introduced them to the concept of attachment styles, helping Emily understand her anxious tendencies and Mark his more avoidant responses. This framework allowed them to view their interactions through a new lens, fostering empathy and understanding.

Therapy sessions focused on communication strategies that enabled them to express their needs and fears without triggering defensive reactions. For instance, Emily learned to articulate her need for closeness in a way that acknowledged Mark's need for space. Mark, on the other hand, worked on consistently providing reassurance to Emily, which helped alleviate some of her anxieties.

Their therapy involved role-playing exercises where Emily and Mark switched roles. This exercise helped Mark experience the anxiety associated with anxious attachment, and Emily understood the pressure avoidant individuals feel when asked for constant reassurance. These role-plays were pivotal in helping them develop a deeper understanding of each other's emotional landscapes.

As therapy progressed, the couple established a routine that included regular check-ins to discuss their relationship dynamics openly. These check-ins allowed them to address minor issues before they escalated into significant conflicts. Additionally, they implemented a 'reassurance ritual' where Mark would initiate affirmations of commitment and support, which helped mitigate Emily's attachment-related fears.

After several months of therapy, Emily and Mark reported a noticeable improvement in the quality of their relationship. They learned to navigate Emily's anxious attachment tendencies and Mark's avoidant behaviors by fostering an environment of open communication and mutual support. Their story highlights the transformative potential of couples therapy in managing anxious attachment in relationships, providing a roadmap for couples facing similar challenges.

CASE STUDY 3: SELF-HELP SUCCESS

Meet Jamie—a 27-year-old graphic designer whose journey through self-help reveals a compelling story of overcoming anxious attachment. Jamie's experience began when she noticed a pattern in her relationships: constant fear of abandonment, intense need for reassurance, and a tendency to cling to partners, which often pushed them away.

Determined to change, Jamie turned to self-help resources. She started with mindfulness meditation to manage her anxiety and stay present in her relationships rather than spiraling into worry about the future. Jamie set aside time each morning to meditate, which gradually helped her recognize and regulate her emotional responses.

Jamie also explored journaling, another self-help tool that provided emotional clarity. She wrote about her feelings daily, tracing them back to her childhood, where she often felt ignored by her busy single mother. This insight was crucial for Jamie to understand that her attachment behaviors were learned and not an intrinsic part of her character.

With a better grasp of her emotions, Jamie began actively working on building her self-esteem. She engaged in positive self-talk, reminding herself of her worth regardless of others' approval or presence. This practice helped her feel more secure, reducing her reliance on others for validation.

Perhaps the most transformative aspect of Jamie's self-help journey was developing a support network. She joined online forums and local groups where people discussed their struggles with attachment issues. These connections gave her perspective and validation, showing her that she was not alone and that change was possible.

Jamie's story is a testament to the power of self-help in addressing anxious attachment. By combining various strategies and persisting through challenges, she transformed her approach to relationships and, most importantly, how she viewed herself. Her journey illustrates that while the path to change is rarely straight, persistence and self-compassion can guide one toward a more secure attachment style.

CASE STUDY 4: RELAPSE AND RECOVERY

In this case study, we explore the journey of Patrick, who has struggled with anxious attachment throughout his adult life. Patrick's story is particularly compelling because it highlights the challenges of relapse and the potential for recovery.

Patrick initially sought therapy after a series of failed relationships that left him feeling desperate and unworthy. His therapist helped him identify patterns of anxious attachment—constantly seeking approval and reassurance, fear of abandonment, and difficulty trusting partners. Through therapy, Patrick began to understand how his early experiences with his unpredictably attentive parents contributed to these patterns.

After a year of therapy, Patrick felt more secure and entered a new relationship with a supportive partner. However, when they hit a rough patch, old anxieties resurfaced. Patrick reverted to his old habits: constant texting, overthinking, and unwarranted jealousy. Recognizing these signs, he felt disheartened but decided to return to therapy.

This time, he focused on developing resilience and coping strategies for moments of stress and insecurity in his relationship. Patrick and his therapist worked on recognizing his triggers and implementing techniques such as mindfulness and self-soothing. They also revisited his communication skills, emphasizing how to express his needs without fear.

Patrick's partner joined some therapy sessions to better understand his attachment style and learn how to nurture their relationship. This joint effort helped them build a stronger foundation and improved their mutual trust.

Patrick's story is a testament to the fact that relapse does not signify failure but is a part of the journey toward lasting change. His willingness to acknowledge setbacks and seek help is crucial to managing anxious attachment. Recovery is not linear, and Patrick's ongoing commitment to his mental health is crucial for his personal growth and the health of his relationships.

Through Patrick's experience, we see the importance of persistence and the value of therapeutic support in navigating the complexities of anxious attachment. His story offers hope and guidance for others facing similar struggles, showing that improvement and stability are within reach with the right tools and support.

CHAPTER 11
CULTURAL PERSPECTIVES

Exploring how different cultures perceive and handle anxious attachment can be quite enlightening. It's fascinating to see how societal norms and values shape how people form and maintain relationships.

Western cultures, particularly in the United States and much of Europe, place a strong emphasis on individualism, which can sometimes exacerbate feelings of anxious attachment. Parents encourage even very young children to be more autonomous, reflecting values of independence and self-reliance. However, if this is not balanced with adequate emotional support and responsiveness, it can leave children feeling insecure and anxious about seeking help or emotional connection, fearing that their needs might be seen as a sign of weakness or dependency. They might worry excessively about rejection or abandonment because their cultural framework doesn't always provide clear scripts for interdependence and emotional support.

Contrast this with collectivist societies, such as those in

many parts of Asia and Africa, where interdependence is typically more valued. In these cultures, extended family and community often play a more significant role in an individual's life. This can sometimes lead to an increased sensitivity to the needs and responses of others, which, while fostering closeness and connectedness, might also heighten anxiety about the stability of these relationships. Children raised in such environments may become excessively tuned into the moods and behaviors of their caregivers, developing anxious attachments out of fear of disapproval or abandonment. The close-knit nature of relationships might alleviate some fears about abandonment, but it could also lead to heightened sensitivity about maintaining harmony and avoiding conflict within the group.

In Japan, for example, the concept of 'amae' is a behavior that seeks to induce caregiving from others. This is considered a normal part of emotional expression within close relationships. This contrasts sharply with Western notions of independence and might influence the manifestation of anxious attachment in culturally specific ways.

Similarly, in many Middle Eastern cultures, family bonds are incredibly tight, and loyalty to the family comes before individual needs. This can provide a secure base for some. Still, for someone with an anxious attachment style, the intense focus on family unity might also pressure them to suppress their anxieties to avoid causing trouble.

Rapid global shifts in technology and social norms are also creating new cultural dynamics that can contribute to anxious attachment. The prevalence of digital communication, for instance, alters how relationships are formed and maintained, potentially increasing anxiety around communication and connection.

Understanding these cultural nuances is crucial for therapists working with clients from diverse backgrounds and individuals navigating relationships influenced by different cultural expectations. It reminds us that the experience and management of anxious attachment can vary widely depending on cultural context. This insight encourages a more empathetic and tailored approach to addressing attachment issues, recognizing the important impact of cultural influences on personal relationships.

GLOBAL VARIATIONS IN THERAPY APPROACHES

Treatment approaches to anxious attachment across different cultures are as diverse as the cultures themselves. Each region has developed unique methods that reflect its societal values, beliefs, and available resources.

In Western countries, therapy often leans towards cognitive-behavioral techniques, which focus on identifying and changing negative thought patterns and behaviors. These regions also show a strong preference for individual therapy sessions, emphasizing personal responsibility and self-improvement.

Contrastingly, in many Asian cultures, such as Japan and China, there is a greater emphasis on community and family systems in therapy. Treatments are more likely to involve the family or broader social networks, reflecting the collectivist nature of these societies. There's often a focus on harmonizing interpersonal relationships and integrating traditional practices like mindfulness and meditation.

Community-based approaches are common in less urbanized areas or countries with limited access to mental health resources, such as parts of Africa and South America. These might include group therapy sessions facilitated by community leaders or trained facilitators who focus on building support networks within the community. Such methods are not only cost-effective but also help in reducing the stigma associated with mental health issues by normalizing the conversation around them.

The Middle East has seen a rise in integrating modern psychotherapy techniques with traditional religious and cultural practices. Therapists might incorporate spiritual counseling with psychological strategies, which resonates well with clients because it aligns with their deeply held beliefs and cultural practices.

Each of these global variations in therapy approaches highlights the adaptability and diversity of psychological treatments and demonstrates the importance of cultural sensitivity and customization in therapeutic practices. It's a vivid reminder that effective therapy must consider the whole person, including their cultural background, to truly support healing and growth.

CULTURAL STIGMA AND MENTAL HEALTH

Cultural stigma plays a significant role in shaping the experiences of individuals with anxious attachment. Across various cultures, the perception and treatment of mental health issues can differ dramatically, often influenced by traditional beliefs, societal norms, and the level of mental health awareness within the community.

For instance, in some cultures, mental health issues are heavily stigmatized, seen as a sign of weakness or as a spiritual failing rather than as medical conditions that require understanding and treatment. This stigma can prevent individuals from seeking help for symptoms of anxious attachment, fearing judgment or ostracization from their community. The fear of being labeled as unstable or incapable can be a powerful deterrent against pursuing therapy or even discussing one's emotional struggles with friends and family.

Moreover, in communities where family and social ties play a central role in an individual's identity, admitting to struggles with anxious attachment can be particularly daunting. Here, the pressure to appear strong and dependable can lead to significant underreporting of attachment issues. This is compounded by the fact that anxious attachment itself can involve heightened fears of rejection and abandonment, making the prospect of facing societal judgment even more intimidating.

Conversely, in societies where there is a greater awareness and acceptance of mental health challenges, individuals might find it somewhat easier to seek help. Educational programs, accessible mental health services, and campaigns that promote mental health awareness contribute to reducing stigma. These environments can empower individuals to address their anxious attachment through therapy, support groups, and other resources without the same level of fear of judgment.

The impact of cultural stigma on mental health is a

complex issue that requires a multifaceted approach. Education plays a crucial role in changing perceptions. By increasing awareness about anxious attachment and its implications, communities can move towards a more empathetic and supportive approach to mental health. This shift helps reduce stigma and encourages a more proactive attitude towards mental wellness, where individuals feel safe to seek help and support.

While the journey towards overcoming cultural stigma is ongoing, understanding its roots and manifestations is a critical step in fostering a more inclusive and supportive environment for individuals dealing with anxious attachment. As cultures evolve and become more interconnected, the hope is that stigma will diminish, making way for more open discussions and better mental health outcomes.

CULTURAL ACCEPTANCE OF SELF-HELP

In some societies, self-help is embraced as a proactive approach to personal development and mental health. These cultures often view self-help as a sign of initiative and strength, encouraging individuals to seek resources such as books, online courses, and community support groups to manage their attachment issues.

In contrast, other cultures might perceive the pursuit of self-help strategies with skepticism or even stigma. In these environments, mental health issues are often seen as matters to be handled within the family or by professionals only. Here, individuals might feel discouraged from seeking self-help solutions due to fear of social judgment or misunderstanding about the nature of anxious attachment.

The resources available for self-help also differ widely across cultures. In countries with more developed mental health services, there is usually a greater availability of self-help books, workshops, and digital content tailored to various aspects of mental health, including anxious attachment. Conversely, in regions where mental health is not as prominently recognized or resourced, there might be fewer available or accessible self-help options.

The internet is changing this landscape dramatically. Online platforms and social media have begun bridging the gap by providing global access to a wealth of self-help information and support networks. This digital revolution allows individuals from less-resourced areas to tap into methods and communities that were previously out of reach, fostering a more inclusive approach to self-help in mental health.

Understanding these cultural nuances is crucial for anyone looking to manage their anxious attachment through self-help. It encourages a sensitive approach that respects cultural contexts and enhances the effectiveness of self-help strategies in diverse settings.

CROSS-CULTURAL RELATIONSHIPS

Navigating cross-cultural relationships can be particularly challenging when one or both partners exhibit signs of anxious attachment. The dynamics of these relationships are influenced not only by individual behaviors and emotional responses but also by the cultural frameworks within which each partner was raised.

In cultures where independence and self-reliance are highly valued, symptoms of anxious attachment, such as needing constant reassurance, may be viewed negatively. On the other hand, in societies where interdependence is emphasized, these behaviors might be more accepted or even expected. This disparity can lead to misunderstandings and conflicts in a relationship where partners come from different cultural backgrounds.

For instance, consider a relationship between a partner from a Western culture, which often prioritizes individualism, and a partner from an Eastern culture, where communal values are more dominant. The Western partner might perceive the Eastern partner's desire for closeness as clinginess or dependency. In contrast, the Eastern partner might view the Western partner's need for space as aloofness or emotional detachment.

Effective communication is vital in these situations. Partners must openly discuss their expectations, comfort levels, and attachment styles. Understanding the cultural context behind a partner's attachment behaviors can foster empathy and patience.

Therapy or counseling that respects and incorporates elements from both cultural backgrounds can be beneficial. Culturally sensitive therapists can help partners navigate the complexities of anxious attachment by integrating diverse cultural perspectives into their therapeutic approaches.

Ultimately, while anxious attachment can pose challenges in cross-cultural relationships, it also offers an opportunity for growth and deeper understanding between partners. By embracing cultural differences and working through attachment insecurities together, couples can build a stronger, more resilient relationship.

IMMIGRATION AND ATTACHMENT

Immigration can profoundly impact attachment styles, particularly for those with an anxious attachment style. When individuals relocate to a new country, the upheaval can exacerbate feelings of insecurity and fear of abandonment, which are hallmarks of anxious attachment. This section explores how immigration can influence these attachment patterns and offers insights into managing these effects.

Imagine moving to a new country where everything from the language to social norms feels alien. For someone with an anxious attachment style, this new environment can trigger intense fears of isolation and rejection. Losing familiar support systems heightens these anxieties, making it challenging to form new, secure attachments.

However, immigration also presents an opportunity for growth and healing. It can serve as a catalyst for individuals to seek out new relationships and support systems that reinforce security and attachment. Engaging with culturally diverse communities can provide a broader perspective and help mitigate the fears associated with anxious attachment.

Support groups and therapy tailored to immigrants can be particularly beneficial. These resources can help individuals understand and navigate the unique challenges posed by their new environment while addressing the root causes of their anxious attachment. By fostering a sense of community and belonging, immigrants can develop healthier attachment patterns, even in the face of initial dislocation.

Understanding the cultural context of the host country can play a crucial role in this adjustment process. Cultural norms around relationships and social interactions can differ significantly from one's country of origin. By learning about these norms, immigrants with anxious attachment can better manage their expectations and interactions, reducing feelings of anxiety and helping them build more secure relationships.

While immigration can intensify the challenges faced by those with anxious attachment, it also offers a unique pathway to overcoming these issues. Through support, cultural understanding, and proactive engagement with their new community, immigrants can transform their attachment experiences and foster a sense of security in their new home.

CHAPTER SUMMARY

- Different cultures handle anxious attachment in unique ways, influenced by societal norms and values.
- Western cultures emphasize individualism, which may increase feelings of insecurity in those with anxious attachment styles.
- Collectivist societies, like in Asia and Africa, value interdependence, potentially alleviating fears of abandonment but increasing sensitivity to group harmony.
- Middle Eastern cultures prioritize tight family bonds, which can pressure individuals with anxious attachment to suppress their anxieties.

- Cultural stigma around mental health varies, affecting how individuals with anxious attachment seek help.
- Therapy approaches differ globally, with Western methods favoring cognitive-behavioral techniques and Eastern methods focusing on community and family systems.
- Self-help acceptance and resources vary by culture, with digital platforms providing more global access to support.
- Cross-cultural relationships can be particularly challenging when one or both partners exhibit signs of anxious attachment because they are influenced by the cultural frameworks within which each partner was raised.

CHAPTER 12
FUTURE DIRECTIONS

As we look toward the future of research in anxious attachment, several promising trends are emerging that could deepen our understanding and improve interventions. The focus is shifting from merely observing behaviors to understanding the underlying neurobiological processes contributing to anxious attachment styles. This involves sophisticated imaging techniques and genetic profiling that can help identify biological markers linked to these attachment styles.

Another exciting area of research is the interplay between genetics and environment. Studies are increasingly looking at how specific environmental factors, such as parenting styles or early childhood trauma, interact with genetic predispositions to influence attachment styles. This research is crucial because it has the potential to lead to personalized therapeutic approaches that consider both genetic makeup and personal history.

Technology, too, is playing a larger role in research and

therapy. Virtual reality (VR) and artificial intelligence (AI) offer new ways to simulate social interactions and environments that can be controlled and manipulated to study behaviors in anxious attachment more closely. These technologies also offer new modalities for therapy, such as VR-based exposure therapy or AI-driven behavioral interventions, which could be tailored to individual needs.

Longitudinal studies are also gaining traction. These studies shed light on how attachment styles evolve over a lifetime and impact various life outcomes. They are particularly valuable as they provide insights not just into the stability of attachment styles but also into the factors that might predict shifts from one style to another, offering hope and direction for those seeking change.

Finally, there is a growing recognition of the need for culturally sensitive research approaches that consider how different cultural backgrounds influence the expression and consequences of anxious attachment. This research expands our understanding of attachment across diverse populations, leading to more inclusive and effective therapeutic approaches.

These research trends promise to enhance our theoretical understanding of anxious attachment and pave the way for more effective and personalized interventions that could help individuals lead healthier, more fulfilling lives.

INNOVATIVE THERAPIES

The field of psychology is buzzing with innovative therapies that promise more personalized and effective interventions. One emerging therapy involves integrating technology with traditional therapeutic techniques, such as virtual reality (VR) environments that simulate real-life interactions for individuals to practice new behaviors in a safe space. This method has shown potential not only in reducing anxiety but also in helping individuals understand and reshape their attachment behaviors.

Another promising approach is the use of biofeedback mechanisms. This therapy involves using real-time displays of brain activity to teach individuals about self-regulation of brain functions. By observing their brain's response to various thoughts and feelings, patients can learn to control their anxious attachments more consciously.

Genetic testing is also becoming a popular component of personalized treatment plans. By understanding the genetic predispositions that contribute to anxious attachment styles, therapists can tailor interventions that are more aligned with the individual's biological makeup, enhancing the effectiveness of the treatment.

On a more personal note, I remember sitting across from a therapist who was explaining the concept of neuroplasticity to me. It was a revelation—the idea that our brains can change and adapt gave me hope. It made me think about the endless possibilities for those struggling with anxious attachment to reshape their thinking patterns.

These innovative therapies are not just about managing symptoms but are aimed at fundamentally changing the way individuals with anxious attachment styles experience and navigate their world. The shift towards more customized and scientifically-backed treatments holds great promise for providing lasting change and a better quality of life for those affected. As we continue to explore and refine these therapies, the future looks hopeful for individuals grappling with the challenges of anxious attachment.

TECHNOLOGY AND MENTAL HEALTH

Technology stands out as a pivotal tool in reshaping mental health practices. Integrating digital platforms into therapeutic settings is not just a trend but a transformation that could democratize access to mental health resources, making them more available and affordable.

One of the most promising technological advancements is the development of mobile apps designed to help individuals manage their anxiety and attachment issues. These apps often include features like mood tracking, mindfulness exercises, and cognitive-behavioral therapy techniques. By regularly using these tools, individuals can gain insights into their emotional patterns and triggers, which is crucial for those with anxious attachment styles.

Teletherapy has also surged in popularity, especially highlighted by the global shift during the COVID-19 pandemic. This mode of therapy allows individuals to connect with mental health professionals via video calls, chats, or phone calls, eliminating geographical barriers. For someone with anxious attachment, the constant availability of their therapist through digital means can provide a sense of security and continuity in care.

Artificial intelligence (AI) is another frontier. AI can personalize mental health care, adapting interventions based on the user's interactions and progress. For instance, AI-driven chatbots can provide immediate support and guidance, mimicking some aspects of therapeutic interactions. This can be particularly beneficial for those who might feel too overwhelmed to seek face-to-face counseling.

However, while technological tools offer significant benefits, they are not without challenges. Issues such as data privacy, the need for human empathy in therapy, and the potential for over-reliance on technology must be carefully navigated. Ensuring these tools are used ethically and effectively will be crucial as we continue integrating technology into mental health care.

The future of technology in the context of addressing anxious attachment looks promising. It can make mental health care more accessible, efficient, and tailored to individual needs. As we advance, it will be vital to balance technological innovations with the irreplaceable human touch at the heart of effective therapy.

EDUCATIONAL PROGRAMS

Educational programs stand out as a pivotal development area for managing anxious attachment. These programs aren't just about spreading awareness; they're about equipping individuals, educators, and mental health professionals with the tools they need to foster secure attachments from early childhood through adulthood.

Imagine a world where school curriculums include modules on understanding and managing different attachment styles. These programs would not only explain the characteristics of anxious attachment but also teach coping strategies that children can use to manage their anxieties and fears. By integrating this knowledge into the educational system, we can help children develop healthier relationships and emotional patterns from a young age.

These educational initiatives could extend beyond the classroom. Workshops for parents and guardians are equally essential, as they often play the most direct role in shaping a child's attachment style. Educating parents about the signs of anxious attachment and effective parenting strategies can prevent or mitigate this attachment style in their children.

In higher education, psychology and counseling courses could include specialized attachment theory training, focusing on practical applications. This would prepare future therapists and counselors to better support clients with anxious attachments, using evidence-based strategies to promote security and resilience.

Community centers and online platforms could offer resources and workshops accessible to everyone, not just students and professionals. These resources could help demystify anxious attachment for the general public, promoting a broader understanding and reducing the stigma associated with attachment issues.

Investing in educational programs at multiple levels can create a ripple effect that enhances societal mental health literacy, reduces the prevalence of anxious attachment, and supports individuals in building stronger, healthier relationships.

POLICY AND MENTAL HEALTH

It's essential to consider the role of policy in shaping effective support systems for anxious attachment. The intersection of policy and mental health is a critical area where progress can be made to enhance the well-being of individuals with anxious attachment styles.

Firstly, there's a pressing need for policies that mandate the integration of attachment theory into the training of all mental health professionals. This would ensure that therapists, counselors, and psychologists have a deep understanding of how attachment styles influence mental health and interpersonal relationships. By being well-versed in attachment theory, professionals can better tailor their interventions to meet the needs of those with anxious attachment.

Public health policies could greatly benefit from incorporating awareness campaigns that educate the community about attachment styles and their impact. Many people suffer from the effects of anxious attachment without ever understanding the root of their struggles. Awareness campaigns help individuals recognize signs of anxious attachment in themselves and others, encouraging them to seek appropriate help sooner.

Another policy direction involves funding research focused explicitly on anxious attachment. While attachment theory is a well-established area of psychology, targeted research on anxious attachment could lead to more specialized interventions. Policies that allocate funds for such research could drive innovations in therapy and support mechanisms, potentially leading to breakthroughs in treatment strategies.

Furthermore, considering the workplace implications of anxious attachment, policies promoting mental health support within the corporate sector are essential. Employers could be encouraged to provide resources like in-house counseling and flexible work arrangements for employees struggling with mental health issues related to attachment styles. Such policies support individual employees and enhance overall productivity and workplace harmony.

Lastly, it's crucial for policies to support school-based programs that address early attachment issues. Interventions at a young age can prevent the escalation of attachment-related problems. Schools play a pivotal role in early detection and intervention, and policies that equip schools with the necessary resources to support children's mental health can have long-lasting positive effects.

The integration of thoughtful, informed policies can significantly alter the landscape of mental health care for individuals with anxious attachment. By focusing on education, professional training, research, workplace support, and early intervention, we can build a more supportive and understanding society that addresses anxious attachment's complexities.

GLOBAL MENTAL HEALTH INITIATIVES

Global mental health initiatives are increasingly recognizing the importance of addressing anxious attachment across populations. These initiatives are not just about spreading awareness; they're about creating actionable, culturally sensitive strategies that can be implemented worldwide.

One of the most promising aspects of these global efforts is the collaboration between countries to share research, resources, and best practices. By pooling knowledge from various cultural backgrounds, mental health professionals can develop more effective interventions that respect and incorporate local traditions and beliefs.

Technology plays a pivotal role in these initiatives. Teletherapy and mobile health apps are breaking down barriers to access, allowing individuals in remote or underserved areas to receive support for anxious attachment issues. These technologies also facilitate international research collaborations and data collection, enhancing our understanding of anxious attachment in different cultural contexts.

Another critical component is the training of local mental health professionals. By increasing the number of trained counselors and therapists in communities worldwide, especially in low-resource settings, we can ensure that more people can access the help they need. This training often includes adapting therapeutic techniques to fit the local cultural context, which is crucial for effective treatment.

Global mental health initiatives also focus on policy-making. Governments are being urged to recognize the impact of attachment disorders like anxious attachment on overall health and to integrate strategies for addressing these issues into public health policies. This includes funding for mental health services and research, as well as policies supporting family and community structures vital for healthy attachment development.

Lastly, these initiatives emphasize the importance of community-based approaches. This involves educating communities about the signs and impacts of anxious attachment and empowering them to support affected individuals. Community leaders, educators, and healthcare providers are trained to recognize anxious attachment behaviors and to provide guidance and referrals to appropriate services.

Through these different strategies, global mental health

initiatives are setting the stage for a future where anxious attachment and other mental health challenges are addressed with the empathy, expertise, and cultural competence they require. This helps individuals heal and thrive and contributes to healthier, more resilient global communities.

CHAPTER SUMMARY

- Research in anxious attachment focuses on neurobiological processes using imaging techniques and genetic profiling to identify biological markers.
- Studies are exploring how environmental factors like parenting styles and early trauma interact with genetics to influence attachment styles, aiming for personalized therapies.
- Virtual reality (VR) and artificial intelligence (AI) are being integrated into research and therapy, offering new ways to simulate social interactions and provide tailored therapeutic interventions.
- There is an increasing emphasis on culturally sensitive research to understand how different cultural backgrounds affect anxious attachment, leading to more inclusive therapies.
- Innovative therapies include VR for real-life simulation, biofeedback to teach self-regulation, and genetic testing to personalize treatment plans based on an individual's biological makeup.

- Technological advancements in mental health care, such as mobile apps for anxiety management and teletherapy, are making mental health resources more accessible and tailored to individual needs.
- Educational programs should be developed to teach about attachment styles from early childhood through adulthood, aiming to foster secure attachments and improve societal mental health literacy.
- Thoughtful, informed policies can alter the landscape of mental health care for individuals with anxious attachment in areas such as education, professional training, research, workplace support, and early intervention.

EPILOGUE

As we reach the concluding chapter of the book, let's revisit the essential insights we've uncovered throughout our journey together.

Firstly, we delved into the roots of anxious attachment, identifying factors such as inconsistent parenting, early childhood experiences, and genetic predispositions. Understanding these origins is crucial for anyone seeking to comprehend their attachment behaviors or those of others.

We then examined the manifestations of anxious attachment in various relationships—from romantic partnerships to friendships and workplace interactions. The common thread across these scenarios is the heightened need for reassurance and the struggle with insecurity and jealousy, which can strain interactions and connections.

Therapeutic approaches like Cognitive Behavioral Therapy (CBT), Dialectical Behavior Therapy (DBT), and Psychodynamic Therapy have been highlighted as effective in managing and potentially altering these attachment patterns. Coupled with self-help strategies such as mindfulness, journaling, and establishing healthy boundaries, individuals have a robust toolkit to foster better self-understanding and improve their relational environments.

Our exploration extended beyond individual experiences to consider cultural influences on attachment. Recognizing the diverse expressions of attachment across different cultures and the unique challenges posed by cultural stigma around mental health is vital for a holistic understanding of anxious attachment.

The personal stories and case studies shared in this book reveal the profound impact of professional intervention and personal effort in navigating the complexities of anxious attachment. These stories offer hope and tangible paths forward for those affected by anxious attachment.

While anxious attachment can pose significant challenges, the growth and healing pathways are varied and accessible. With the right support and strategies, transformation is not just possible but achievable.

YOUR NEXT STEPS

Take a moment to recognize the courage it takes to embark on a journey of self-discovery and healing. Understanding and addressing anxious attachment is not just about managing symptoms—it's about transforming your relationship with yourself and others.

There will be days filled with breakthroughs and days when old patterns seem to resurface. This is all part of the healing process. No matter how small, each step is a step towards a more secure and fulfilled you.

Embrace the tools and strategies discussed throughout this book. Whether through therapy, self-help techniques, or simply becoming more mindful in daily interactions, each effort is a building block toward a healthier attachment style. Lean on your support networks, and don't hesitate to seek help. There is strength in vulnerability.

As you move forward, remember that change is possible. Your past does not have to dictate your future. Patience and persistence can reshape your attachment style and build deeper, more satisfying connections.

So, take a deep breath and step forward with hope. Your journey toward attachment security is a brave and rewarding endeavor. Celebrate each victory, learn from the challenges, and continue to grow. You are not alone on this path.

CONTINUING EDUCATION AND AWARENESS

Understanding and managing anxious attachment is not a one-time task but a continuous journey that evolves with new research and societal changes.

Continuing education in the realm of anxious attachment can take many forms. Staying updated with the latest research through journals, workshops, and seminars is essential for professionals in psychology and therapy. This not only enhances their therapeutic skills but also ensures they provide the most effective strategies to those struggling with anxious attachment.

Whether you identify with having an anxious attachment style or know someone who does, ongoing learning can be incredibly empowering. Books, articles, podcasts, and videos are great resources that can offer new insights and coping strategies. They can help you understand the nuances of your attachment style and how it affects your relationships.

Awareness is equally important. It involves recognizing the signs of anxious attachment in oneself and relationships. Awareness also means advocating for mental health and reducing the stigma around attachment issues. By openly discussing these topics, we can foster a supportive community where seeking help and sharing experiences is normalized and encouraged.

As you continue to learn and grow, keep an open mind and be compassionate towards yourself and others. The journey may be challenging, but it is also filled with opportunities for personal development and deeper connections.

THE IMPORTANCE OF COMMUNITY SUPPORT

Navigating anxious attachment can often feel like a solitary journey. However, the role of community support in this process is fundamental. When individuals with anxious attachment styles connect with supportive communities, they find not only a safe space to share their experiences but also access to a wealth of collective wisdom and coping strategies.

Community support provides a unique form of validation that is crucial for those dealing with anxious attachment. It reassures them that they are not alone in their struggles. This sense of belonging can significantly diminish feelings of isolation often accompanying this attachment style.

Support extends beyond emotional reassurance. It

provides practical tools and resources that can be pivotal in managing anxious attachment. For instance, workshops on building and maintaining healthy relationships, lectures on self-care practices, and group therapy sessions are common offerings that can equip individuals with the skills needed to improve their interpersonal dynamics.

While the journey towards overcoming anxious attachment is deeply personal, it doesn't need to be lonely. The collective strength of a supportive community can light the path toward healing and hope, making the challenges of anxious attachment more manageable and less intimidating.

FINAL THOUGHTS

Understanding anxious attachment is more than just recognizing a pattern—it's about embracing the complexity of human connections and their lasting impact on our lives.

Anxious attachment shapes how we view ourselves and interact with others. It's a lens through which many see our world, often colored by fear and a craving for security. But as we've discovered, it's not an unchangeable fate. The pathways to healing and growth are numerous and varied, each offering a chance to rewrite the narratives of our relationships.

The journey toward secure attachment is neither quick nor easy, but it is filled with potential for personal transformation. It requires courage to confront and work through deep-seated fears and insecurities. Yet, the rewards—healthier relationships, improved self-esteem, and a more stable emotional landscape—are invaluable.

The tools and knowledge you've gained from this book

are your companions on this journey. Use them to guide you, to find support, and to remind yourself of your strengths and capabilities.

Thank you for taking this journey with me. May it kick-start a lifelong quest toward understanding, healing, and genuine connection.

ACKNOWLEDGMENTS

As we reach the end of this book, I am filled with immense gratitude for the numerous individuals who have contributed to its creation and completion.

Firstly, a heartfelt thank you to the mental health professionals whose insights and expertise have been invaluable in the writing of this book. Their willingness to share knowledge and experiences has enriched the content significantly, providing a solid foundation for understanding and addressing anxious attachment.

I also deeply appreciate the individuals who bravely shared their personal stories. Your experiences have illuminated the real-world implications of anxious attachment and provided hope and inspiration to others facing similar challenges.

A special thanks to my editor, whose keen eye and thoughtful suggestions have helped shape this manuscript into a clearer, more impactful resource. Your guidance was crucial at every step of the writing process.

To the research teams and academic contributors who provided the latest studies and findings, your rigorous work and dedication to advancing our understanding of attachment theory are profoundly respected and have been critical in offering the most current information.

I must also acknowledge my family and friends for their unwavering support and patience throughout the creation of this book. Your encouragement and belief in the importance of this work have been a constant source of motivation.

Lastly, thank you, dear readers. Thank you for trusting this resource. May it serve as a stepping stone towards greater self-awareness and healthier relationships.

Together, we continue to learn, grow, and support one another in our journeys toward attachment security and emotional well-being. Thank you for being an integral part of this important conversation.

YOUR FEEDBACK MATTERS

As we reach the end of this book, I extend my heartfelt gratitude for your time and engagement. It's been an honor to share this journey with you, and I hope it has been as enriching for you as it has been for me.

Your feedback helps me as an independent author and guides fellow readers searching for their next meaningful read. Your insights and reflections are invaluable to me. By sharing them, you contribute to a larger conversation that extends far beyond the pages of this book.

If the ideas we've explored have sparked new thoughts, inspired change, or provided comfort, I'd really appreciate it if you could share your experience with others by leaving a review on the platform on which you purchased this book. Alternatively, you can follow the QR code below.

Thank you once again for your company on this literary adventure. May the insights you've gained stay with you, and may your quest for knowledge be ever-fulfilling.

ABOUT THE AUTHOR

Laura Collins is a passionate author and expert in the field of psychology. With a robust academic background and years of practical experience, Laura brings a wealth of knowledge to her writing, particularly in the realm of attachment theory.

Her insights into the complex dynamics of human relationships are reflected in her evocative and accessible books for adults. Laura's work not only demystifies the intricacies of attachment theory but also offers practical strategies for personal growth and healthier connections.

Her thoughtful prose and empathetic approach have made her a trusted voice for readers seeking to understand and overcome the anxieties that can undermine their relationships. Whether you want to enhance your emotional intelligence or navigate the nuances of attachment in your own life, Laura's books provide valuable guidance and transformative insights.

www.ingramcontent.com/pod-product-compliance
Lightning Source LLC
Chambersburg PA
CBHW071714020426
42333CB00017B/2265